Spirit Guides

The Ultimate Guide to Contacting and Communicating with Your Guardian Angels, Spirit Animals, Archangels, and More

© Copyright 2022 - All rights reserved.

The content contained within this book may not be reproduced, duplicated, or transmitted without direct written permission from the author or the publisher.

Under no circumstances will any blame or legal responsibility be held against the publisher, or author, for any damages, reparation, or monetary loss due to the information contained within this book, either directly or indirectly.

Legal Notice:

This book is copyright protected. It is only for personal use. You cannot amend, distribute, sell, use, quote, or paraphrase any part, or the content within this book, without the consent of the author or publisher.

Disclaimer Notice:

Please note the information contained within this document is for educational and entertainment purposes only. All effort has been executed to present accurate, up-to-date, reliable, and complete information. No warranties of any kind are declared or implied. Readers acknowledge that the author is not engaging in the rendering of legal, financial, medical, or professional advice. The content within this book has been derived from various sources. Please consult a licensed professional before attempting any techniques outlined in this book.

By reading this document, the reader agrees that under no circumstances is the author responsible for any losses, direct or indirect, that are incurred as a result of the use of the information contained within this document, including, but not limited to, errors, omissions, or inaccuracies.

Free Bonus from Silvia Hill available for limited time

Hi Spirituality Lovers!

My name is Silvia Hill, and first off, I want to THANK YOU for reading my book.

Now you have a chance to join my exclusive spirituality email list so you can get the ebooks below for free as well as the potential to get more spirituality ebooks for free! Simply click the link below to join.

P.S. Remember that it's 100% free to join the list.

~~$27~~ FREE BONUSES

- 9 Types of Spirit Guides and How to Connect to Them
- How to Develop Your Intuition: 7 Secrets for Psychic Development and Tarot Reading
- Tarot Reading Secrets for Love, Career, and General Messages

Access your free bonuses here
https://livetolearn.lpages.co/spirit-guides-paperback/

Table of Contents

INTRODUCTION	1
CHAPTER ONE: WHAT IS A SPIRIT GUIDE?	3
CHAPTER TWO: GETTING IN TOUCH WITH YOUR ANCESTORS	14
CHAPTER THREE: ASCENDED MASTERS AND HISTORICAL FIGURES	25
CHAPTER FOUR: ELEMENTAL BEINGS AND NATURE SPIRITS	32
CHAPTER FIVE: WORKING WITH SPIRIT ANIMALS	40
CHAPTER SIX: DEITIES AS SPIRIT GUIDES	48
CHAPTER SEVEN: UNDERSTANDING ANGELS AND ARCHANGELS	56
CHAPTER EIGHT: CONTACT YOUR GUARDIAN ANGEL	64
CHAPTER NINE: WORKING WITH ARCHANGELS	72
CHAPTER TEN: OTHER GUIDES AND HOW TO FIND THEM	83
CONCLUSION	93
HERE'S ANOTHER BOOK BY SILVIA HILL THAT YOU MIGHT LIKE	95
FREE BONUS FROM SILVIA HILL AVAILABLE FOR LIMITED TIME	96
REFERENCES	97

Introduction

Suppose you've ever been interested in the spirit realm. In that case, you may be aware of a theory that claims we all have spirit guides — an embodiment of our higher selves —constantly watching over us. Not only do these guides provide a source of direction and guidance for your life, but they also offer protection from negative entities. For the average person, contact with their spirit guide is fairly sporadic, but there are ways to increase your chances of connecting with them.

There are a couple of advantages to connecting with your spirit guides. As mentioned, there is the practical issue of guidance and protection, but it's also possible that there are healing benefits involved. Another reason this is an endeavor worth looking into is that when you connect with them regularly, you'll receive the simple assurance that they will watch over you. They'll be able to provide you with a higher perspective on life in general.

You'll find that this is a practical guidebook that will take you by the hand and walk you through the process of finding and connecting with your spirit guides. It's a book that is very much needed in today's world, where things are very uncertain, and it's hard to find your way through your life with everything thrown at us by the modern world. You'll learn how to connect with all sorts of spirit helpers, from archangels to spirit animals, guardian angels, and more.

Fortunately, you've chosen just the right book. It's written in clear and simple English, doing away with any terminologies that may make it difficult for those with non-specialized knowledge on spiritual matters to connect with the concepts explained. You'll find that it has enough exercises and practical, hands-on techniques to help you find and connect with your personal guides. Unlike other books out there, this book is particularly concerned with keeping you safe all the way through the process, and not only that, but the things you will learn aren't your regular page-one results on Google. You'll also be pleased to note that the writing is deliberately inclusive, so no matter where you're from or how you identify, you can trust that you will be treated with respect from page one through to the end.

It doesn't matter if you're a complete novice regarding spiritual affairs or if you've been on your spiritual path for many years. In the pages of this book, there is something for one and all, and you're bound to find it a rich addition to your knowledge bank on spiritual matters. Every chapter has some golden nugget of wisdom that could change your life phenomenally if you allow it.

Rather than being a cold, clinical dissection of methods required to make contact with the spirit realm, this book is warm and packed with stories of how ordinary people like you could connect with their guides. People who have had very real experiences with them. Allow their stories to inspire you and give you the faith you need to make it happen for you. If you're ready to make the incredible journey toward connecting with those charged with keeping you safe, loved, protected, and provided for, then let's get started.

Chapter One: What Is a Spirit Guide?

You're never alone. Even when you feel at your loneliest, there's always someone with you, whether you know it or not. There could be one or more beings with you, but there's never a moment when you're left to your own devices. The trouble is that many people don't know how to contact these spiritual friends - deliberately - to ask for their help, and that's what you will learn to do in this book. Who are these friends, ready to assist you in any way they can? They are your spirit guides.

What is a spirit guide? A spirit guide is any being or entity in the spiritual realm who can make their presence known in our world, so they can offer us help, support, insight, guidance, miracles, and protection from harm. These beings will offer their guidance through subtle spiritual means like intuition, dreams, and visions. Sometimes, they can make themselves visible so that you can observe them with your own eyes.

Your spirit guide can take on so many forms, but, in the end, it is helpful to think of them from an energetic standpoint. The form they take on is usually chosen to help you connect with them in the way only you can or to help you glean a specific message that wouldn't strike you deeply any other way. Sometimes they can show up as regular people, with the only telltale signs that they're not regular people being the way they showed up, helped you with something, and promptly faded into the background.

This book seeks to answer the question, how can you connect with your guides deliberately and make communion with them an everyday thing? This question is worth answering because when you choose to become more aware of your guides, you will find that they, in turn, will improve your quality of life.

Spirit Guides in the World's Religions

Most major religions include a belief in spirit guides. Some of them, like angels, are pretty obvious. However, other traditions describe their guides as more subtle and ambiguous entities. In Buddhism, for instance, the concept of spirit guides is known as the "spirit teacher." This source of wisdom can help a person overcome suffering by learning to accept change and relinquish human attachments to material possessions. The "spirit teacher" can guide a person toward enlightenment and help them to develop the correct principles for living a fulfilled life.

In Hinduism, there are numerous spirit guides known as *Acharyas*. These are minor deities that serve to protect people from harm. They also act as divine advisers and teachers for the gods. They're similar to angels in that they do not possess their own form but have unique personalities. Similar concepts are found in Christianity, with the concept of guardian angels and, for the most part, spirit guides that protect people from demonic influence.

In Islam, the angel Jibra'il is considered a spirit guide who helps people develop their spirituality and find inner peace. In Judaism, there are angels known as *malakim*. These spirits also serve to help people to overcome suffering and develop correct principles for living. They can provide a source of guidance and an idea of how they want to be remembered in death.

The possession of a spirit guide is not an uncommon concept in the New Age community. This belief has its roots in 19th-century Spiritualism, which was largely purveyed by people who believed they could communicate with the dead. This remains a popular belief today, particularly among people who practice mediumship or contact spirits to help someone else.

Does the idea of spirit guides sound far-fetched? Well, if you're willing to entertain the notion that humans are capable of communicating with the dead, then how much more logical is it to believe that we can communicate with our own spirits? Although traditional religions may not accept this belief, that doesn't necessarily mean it's wrong. After all, there's no way to prove whether angels and other entities exist in any objective scientific sense. However, when you look at it from the point of view of personal experience and subjective evidence - particularly in the form of meditative or prayer experiences - it is easy to see how this concept can be taken seriously.

Returning to the idea that contact with your spirit guides can protect you from harm, there is some scientific backing for this viewpoint. Scientific studies have found that prayer provides comfort, security, and a greater likelihood of overcoming challenges such as illness or addiction.

The Roles of Spirit Guides

1. **They help you figure out what your purpose in life is.** We all have moments in our lives when we question the purpose of life. We wonder if we're here to do anything specific or if we're only born to distract ourselves until we die. Whenever you're feeling that sense of existential crisis, you can rest assured that having access to your spirit guides will help you understand your purpose in life. They can help you find peace because you're exactly where you need to be. If you want to know what the next step is for you in life, you can trust them to set things up so that you will know just what to do. They help plant you in the right place at the right time to accomplish what you came here for.

2. **They keep you safe and protected.** One of the most common reasons to get in touch with your spirit guides is to ask them for protection. As mentioned earlier, they guard us against negative influences and help us avoid those things that could harm us. From a more practical viewpoint, this means they help keep you out of trouble when you come into contact with people or situations

that could put you in danger. They can also assist you when trying to set up your life for success by helping you steer clear of risk-taking behavior or anything else that might stand in the way.

3. **They provide gifts or inspiration.** It's not a bad idea to ask your spirit guides for gifts or inspiration since this is one of the main functions they're meant to play in our lives. If you're working on a big project or goal, it's usually a good idea to reach out to them and ask them what they think of your chances of success. They can work as advisors in decision-making since they'll have something to say about whether something will work out based on their own experiences. They can also serve as a sounding board for your long-term goals and plans to get a view of your direction instead of just going by your feelings. This can help you stay on course when things turn for the worst and ensure you don't veer off course.

4. **They encourage you to set and achieve goals.** One thing we often forget about is how important it is to have goals in life. Goals keep us motivated since they're meant to be our motivation system. This doesn't mean that, without spirit guides, we'd be left without goals. But it's always helpful to have a little peer pressure and support behind you. Spirit guides tend to be very encouraging by nature. They're great at helping you create big goals and keep you motivated to achieve them.

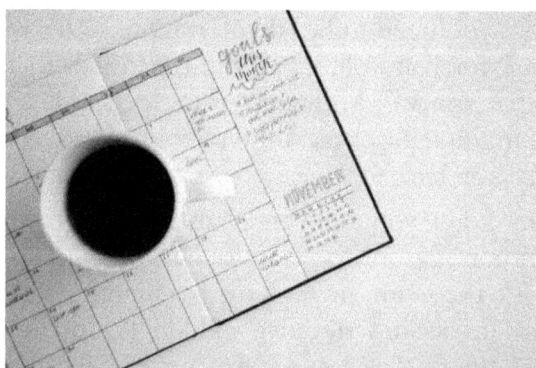

Spirit guides encourage you to set and achieve your goals.
https://unsplash.com/photos/aQfhbxailCs?utm_source=unsplash&utm_medium=referral&utm_content=creditShareLink

5. **They can heal you.** This one is pretty obvious, but it's still important. Spirit guides can assist in healing, both emotionally and physically. This can include relieving stress, reducing anxiety, helping you sleep better, or even curing physical illnesses. This depends on the type of spirit guide you're talking to. For example, suppose you're working with a guide who specializes in healing. In that case, it will be easier for them to help you through your problems than if you were working with laid-back energy who's more focused on socializing. They may also know exactly who you need to see or what information you need to learn to access the healing you seek. This may mean you'll get a message from them to see someone because they think you need treatment for an illness or an injury, even before it happens.
6. **They help you get over obstacles.** Everyone has obstacles in life, and the trick is to find a way to deal with them. If you have a problem at work or a relationship issue, reaching out to your guides can be an effective way to deal with that problem. Guides specializing in heart issues can provide advice on how to get over your ex, fix issues at work, or help you learn better ways to deal with people in general. This is why ensuring you work with a knowledgeable guide is important.
7. **They can help you to meditate.** It's been said that spirit guides specialize in meditation, and they can be very helpful to those who know how to work with them. Since this skill is one of the most powerful tools available for dealing with any issue, you must prioritize learning how to use mediation to manage your life and heal yourself. Meditation puts you in a state where you're not only able to connect with your guides more efficiently, but you can also accept the spiritual and physical miracles waiting for you to receive them.

Signs Your Spirit Guide Is Around

1. **You feel a constant emotional pull.** You may just be going about your business when you're hit with a very strong emotion that you can't justify. This is one way your spirit guide can reach out to get your attention. The emotion you feel could be so intense that you feel a pain deep in your chest, a wave of giddy excitement, or some strong movement of energy in your solar plexus. You could also suddenly get goosebumps as a result of those strong emotions they create within you. Try to recall whatever you were thinking about, or consider who you were talking to or the situation you're in. They may be trying to tell you something about it. Notice the quality of the emotion as well, and act accordingly. Here's Kate's story: *"I was in the parking lot at the mall about to enter my car when I felt a sudden strong feeling in my chest, almost like pain. I couldn't explain it, but it was followed by a strong urge to go back into a certain store. So, I did just that, and there I found a little girl who had lost her mom and was looking scared. I asked her what her mother was wearing, and she mentioned she'd had a gray shirt with blue jeans. Several people were dressed that way, but I got the same tug in my chest again, followed by an urge to look up. I saw a woman who fit the description, and I just knew it was her. The little girl confirmed it, and the woman was happy to be reunited with her kid again."*

2. **You see physical signs.** Your guides can also make their presence known through things like signs. This can be anything you could interpret as a sign, like a set of numbers or even words on a piece of paper or billboard. Often, people will dismiss these signs as nothing more than mere coincidence, but that's not the case. This is synchronicity, one of the languages your spirit guides will use to connect with you. They could make you pass by strangers talking about something you were just thinking about, bring your attention to clocks and license plates

when they show certain numbers, or wake you up at very specific times during the night. When these things happen, you should know that your guides are near and may have some important information to share with you. You may also notice flashes, shimmering lights, and a presence just outside your line of sight that seems to hover behind you, among other things. Mark says, "*Every time my spirit guides want to get my attention, I tend to see the number 333 or 212. Often, I find that if I pause to recall what I was thinking about when I saw those numbers, the answer to the problem I was dealing with at that moment blossoms in my mind in the form of a picture. I've learned never to take those signs for granted.*"

3. **You notice others around you react to your guides.** Someone may ask you if you just felt an odd breeze in a still room or if you heard a sound or something. Normally, you should be able to sense these things on your own, but if you're feeling doubtful about the presence of your guide, they could reach out by making their presence known to other people in the room as well. Gwen says, "*My spirit guides like to have a bit of fun with me and the people around me. Often, I could be talking to a friend, and we'd both get a weird chilly sensation on the napes of our necks. My friends have become sufficiently comfortable to joke about it. When that happens, I often stay still and listen to my inner intuition. There's always a message for my friends and me when my guides show up in that way.*"

Your spirit guide is there. You just have to know how to find them. They are always with us and can't be silenced for long periods. If the signs are clear enough, you can feel their presence.

How to Avoid Connecting with the Wrong Spirits

When spirits cross over, they have many reasons for doing so. There are messages they hope to bring up to loved ones or tasks they need to perform. We must treat them with respect and the individual time and attention they require.

However, there are times when a spirit will try to connect with someone who does not want them around for one reason or another. After all, it can be difficult enough for a spirit to find the person they want without being sent on an endless chase due to unwanted connections that the living makes with them, consciously or subconsciously.

Connecting with spirits is not uncommon, but when the wrong kind of spirit comes through, it can be disastrous. You can do the following to avoid connecting with the wrong spirit or to sort things out if you wind up contacting one.

1. **Call a professional exorcist.** If you sense a negative presence, contact a professional who will conduct an exorcism on your person or house. It is important to remove any negative energy present for positive energy to flow freely.
2. **Make sure you have adequate home protection.** Use protective symbols around your house and land if you feel unsafe, and make sure that you do not leave mirrors in front of your bed when you go to sleep so that they don't act as portals for the spirit to invite more spirits to bother you or give you nightmares.
3. **Make personal protection a priority.** Always have a clear mind, stay in a good positive state, and ensure that your spiritual energy is always balanced and in check. Suppose you are feeling unwell or get that feeling that an evil spirit has possessed you. In that case, it is best to immediately seek help from a powerful spiritual person who is experienced in these matters.

4. **Make sure you get protection from your family and get them to protect themselves.** Family members and relatives may be able to feel the presence of a negative spirit. If this is the case, they may be able to identify it and help you rid yourself of it. They also need to protect themselves by becoming more spiritual and doing things like regular cleansing rituals.
5. **Join a support group.** If you are connected with a wrong spirit and would like to connect with the right one, then join a support group on Facebook or in person, where there is an opportunity for you to share your experiences and stories without fear of judgment. This forum allows you to empathize with people in similar situations and exchange advice to safeguard yourself against negative forces when engaging with them.
6. **Have a trusted person in your life you can talk to about it.** It helps to relieve the burden if you can talk about the problem you're facing with someone who is not only close to you but who will not judge you for trying to walk your spiritual path or making a mistake.
7. **Have a personal relationship with the Divine.** Developing a personal relationship with the Universe or your higher power is another way to avoid connecting with the wrong spirits. The source is light, love, and positive energy; therefore, inviting presence into your life will allow positive energy and good spirits to enter while discouraging negative ones from making their home inside you.
8. **Do some self-examination.** If you are connected with the wrong spirit, then you may want to examine why you contacted it in the first place. Things such as revenge, negative thoughts and feelings, depression, and hurt can lead you toward connecting with a negative spirit. Negative spirits will bring out these traits in people they possess to keep themselves happy. Also, if your connection with a negative spirit is self-inflicted, you could have some issues that need to be resolved on your part. This may include deep-rooted childhood issues or other trauma that has not been dealt with properly and manifests through unwanted

haunting or attacks from a supernatural being.

9. **Don't be alarmed if you do connect with a negative spirit.** Do not be alarmed if you are experiencing anything out of the ordinary and feel everything is fine and nothing is happening. Fearing will feed the negative entity and encourage them to stick around and torment you. When you choose to be blasé about their presence and unbothered, this discourages them from seeking you out to make trouble for you, and they could leave you alone eventually.

10. **Disconnect your energy from the negative spirit.** Visualize a cord connecting you, and then visualize yourself encased in pink light. Let this light cut through the cord that connects you to the spirit. Then, imagine the pink ball of light growing brighter and melting the spirit into nothingness. This exercise should be done from a place of love – not fear – if you want it to be effective.

11. **Ask spirits to leave your property.** If you have unwelcome spirits, it is best not to invite them in. It's not just a case of telling them to leave and expecting it all to be over and done with. You need to ask them to go in a respectful but firm way.

12. **Summon your other spirit guides and ask them to banish this negative spirit from your life.** Simply ask them to take the spirit away, and they will do it, as spirit guides are a source of positive energy, and the negative spirit can't abide by their presence. You can also enlist their help to rid you of the negative entity by asking them to surround you and your property with love and light.

13. **Summon Archangel Michael.** Call upon this Archangel by name and request him to come to remove the negative spirit from your midst. He is an angel who is prompt to answer your calls for help and will not let you down. He will remove the entity with his sword of fire, burning it out of your existence.

14. **Sprinkle salt around your home.** Salt is an energetic purifier. If there's one thing negative entities cannot stand, it is salt. You can sprinkle it in corners, at your doors and

windows, and around your bed. Also, when you take a bath, you should do so with some salt. Envision the salty water enveloping you with a purifying, protective white light that keeps you safe from all harm.

15. **Burn some sage**. Sage has always been used by one and all to eliminate unwelcome presences in a space. Its smoke purifies the energy and makes it incredibly difficult for negative spirits and other beings to stick around. So, consider getting some sage from a new age store and smudge your house, working from room to room. Don't just walk around aimlessly. You have to fix the intention in your mind that you want your home to be free of negativity as you smudge it.

16. **Light a white candle and intend for its energy to cleanse your home.** White is a very significant color. It's a color that attracts positive energy. So, if you get the sense that a spirit you invited isn't who you thought it was, and you want to rid yourself of it, you can light a white candle in each room and let it burn out completely. Set the intention in your mind that the candle's energy will drive away all evil and bring only love and peace into your space. Be aware of safety at all times when working with candles.

Chapter Two: Getting in Touch with Your Ancestors

Ancestors and departed loved ones are some of the easiest spirit guides to get in touch with because you share emotional and blood ties with them. Who are your ancestors? We all have a past. We all come from somewhere, and somewhere on that family tree is a figure or figures near and dear to us. We may not know much about them, but they are there and ready to be contacted through the power of intention.

Your ancestors are spirits. They are entities you may have physically or energetically come from, transcending their physical bodies. Because of this, they are much more powerful than most spirits you will come across. Your ancestors could be the spirits of loved ones, friends, relatives, and others connected to your bloodline or generation before they passed away into the spirit realm where they now reside. They are not only there to offer you guidance and love, but they can be extremely useful when it comes to spell work when trying to influence a situation or the actions of another person or being.

The most important thing to remember when trying to reach your ancestors is that you may not always be able to contact the specific spirit you are looking for. Instead, try reaching out specifically to the spirit of your closest bloodline. You may not be able to connect with a specific loved one, but instead with someone who resembles their personality or looks. Your ancestors know what they are doing, and there is a reason why they have come to you in the form they choose. There may be something you need to learn or a specific message they have for you. If your intentions are in the right place, they will come through. They are here as long as you need them, and nothing could make an ancestor prouder than seeing their family members succeeding in life. You may not always be able to see them, but they're very close to you and can communicate with you differently if you stay open to them.

Apart from their general wisdom and knowledge, there are several reasons why contacting your ancestors can be beneficial to you. They can give you advice on anything troubling you. They have been there and done that. They have seen things we could only dream of and have infinite knowledge about everything in the universe.

What Do Your Ancestors Look Like?

Your ancestors can appear to you in your dreams, dressed just as you'd expect them to have been back in their time. Sometimes they may show up wearing all white or whatever color is most associated with your bloodline on an energetic level. You'll know this color, too, because the odds are while it may not be your favorite color, you may have a strong fascination with it, or people may have strong reactions to you when you put it on.

Your ancestors can also show up as nothing more than energy. However, this doesn't mean you won't be able to deduce it's them. You can tell because they will let you know who they are through intuitive nudges or any other means at their disposal (such as someone randomly talking about ancestry or a book falling and opening to a specific page that talks about ancestors and guides).

Signs Your Ancestors Are Around You

It doesn't mean it's the end of life when we pass away. It's a new beginning, and for ancestors, part of that new beginning will involve their old life somehow. This is why they're invested in seeing how their successors are doing in life, and when they can help, they will. We just need to know how to sense their presence and encourage it. So here are the signs that they're trying to reach out to you.

You dream about them: This is one of the ways you can tell your ancestors want to connect with you. They'll come to you in dreams or as actual nightly visions. Spirits who have passed on favor dreams a lot. The nature of these dreams tends to be hyper-realistic, even more real than waking life. Here's Zoe's story: "My dad passed away not too long ago as a result of the pandemic. He and I had had a rocky relationship as far back as I can remember, but toward the end of his life, he'd tried to reach out to make amends. Sadly, I was a little too proud to let him do that, and I felt too hurt by his past actions to be able to forgive him.

"I remember the last message I sent him was that I'd see him eventually. I had no idea how wrong I would be. When he got sick, I was too far away to do anything, and the lockdowns were in full force. Not a day or night went by after that when I wasn't torn up with guilt. Well, one night, I went to bed and had a dream. I saw him, wearing the whitest outfit I'd ever seen, standing at a peaceful, serene river. He smiled beautifully, looking radiant, and beckoned me to join him. He hugged me, and without words, he let me know it was okay. He held nothing against me, was sorry for how he'd been when he was alive and said he would always watch over me. As I hugged him, tears filled my eyes. When I woke up, my body felt as though I really had just been hugging someone, and I smelled his scent of Old Spice, tobacco, and an odd perfume. Since then, I've been reaching out to him for help and companionship, and he's been very good to me."

You get intuitive nudges to take action right away. This is another common experience that tells you it's your ancestors speaking to you. Say you're wondering how you will get a new car when you can't afford one. Your ancestors could cause you to suddenly desire to go through your spam mail, and you might find a message from an old client who wants you to help them with a project that could incidentally net you just enough money to get the car you'd like. So, it goes without saying how important it is to be in tune with your intuition because ancestral spirits can communicate better with you when you're deliberate about listening. In fact, here's a true story about how Nick could get himself out of a toxic relationship thanks to listening to his ancestors. *"I had hoped for years that things would change, but by the time it became evident to me that my partner would always be the same and not make any effort to do better, I was trauma bonded to them. This meant that each time I thought of leaving, I just couldn't bring myself to do that. So, I said a quick, quiet, desperate prayer to my ancestors. It was all of four words: 'Please 'Please set me free.' This led to a series of events where I found out my partner had been unfaithful to me. I wouldn't have found out if I hadn't listened to my ancestors when they told me to call specific people, check specific spots in the house for signs, and so on. I knew what I found wouldn't be enough to convince me to let my partner go, so I said another prayer, 'Please give me the strength to walk away.' Things played out in a matter of days in such a way that whether I wanted to or not, I had to leave. My ancestors led me to a wonderful relationship six months after that. I'm thankful to them."*

Someone says or does something around you that distinctly reminds you of them. Maybe they talk about them, clear their throat just like they used to, or sing a melody that's too obscure for anyone else to know but your ancestor. Here's Shawna's experience of this very phenomenon: *"My mother passed away, and things weren't great where we left them. I had always wondered about what could have been. One day, a friend called me up to tell me about her own mother, who hadn't been good to her either. She told me that her mother had called her out of the blue to say, 'I'm very sorry for never being there for you, but I promise you that from now on, I'm always available to you no matter what.' As she said those words, I felt goosebumps all over me. As if that wasn't enough, the radio I'd had on suddenly went from playing modern music to a song by Tina Turner, which my mother would often sing around the house when we were younger."* For Shawna, this was clearly no accident at all. She had just received communication from her mother through her friend. That's how the ancestors work sometimes.

They could reach out through animals. If your ancestor had a special animal they loved, don't be surprised if you notice them around you a lot or if they tend to stop and funnily stare at you.

You may also suddenly be inclined to have an animal just like theirs or find yourself a sudden parent to one. This could be your ancestors trying to comfort you and show you they still love you and are very present. Sometimes, it may not be actual animals but pictures of them. Many people have stories about how they'd suddenly start seeing cats or owls everywhere they went when they lost a loved one. They talk about seeing them on the television, at the store, or even at work, one of the last places most people expect to run into animals.

Your ancestors can reach out through animals.
https://pixabay.com/images/id-2083492/

Don't assume you never could if you've never had any of these experiences. There are ways to achieve contact with your ancestors, and we'll get to those in a minute, but first, let's talk about how important your family tree is.

Your Ancestral Family Tree

You don't need to know your family tree, as you could simply work with the loved ones you know who have passed on, whether that's a parent, grandparent, aunt, or anyone you had a blood connection with. However, it can be pretty beneficial if you want to work with your ancestors to know your lineage. No mistake about it; figuring out your lineage can be complicated, but it is worth the effort. Fortunately, you can find websites on the Internet that can help you locate your family line and build up your family tree. Knowing your family tree is important because not only can you know the names of the ancestors you want to work with in particular, but also the periods in which they lived and where they originally came from. The more you know about their place and time, traditions and customs, the easier it'll be for you to connect with them.

Apart from websites like Ancestry.com to help you with your family tree, you can also get your DNA analyzed to learn more about your roots. It may surprise you that you may have much more interesting roots than you once assumed. A quick search on the Internet should show you websites that make it possible for you to get an analysis of your DNA and receive your results. Knowing your roots will help you reconstruct the lives and times of your ancestors so that you can form a stronger bond with them.

Before You Reach Out

Reaching out to your ancestors is an endeavor that should be taken with all necessary precautions. The last thing you want to do is have yourself interacting with the trickster spirit masquerading as one of your own. So, before you begin, we need to cover the necessary things you must do to put yourself in the right frame of mind and spirit to connect with your ancestors.

1. **Have a cleansing bath.** This is no ordinary bath as it is meant to rid you of physical, spiritual, and energetic debris from your body and soul. Working with spiritual matters is like attracts like; therefore, if you carry stuck negative energy, you may be attractive to tricksters and negative entities. For this cleansing bath, simply put some salt into your water and intend that you're cleansed, spiritually and physically. If it helps, you can envision yourself being surrounded by white light as you soak in the tub. If you don't have a tub, simply take a regular bath, and then you can burn some sage to cleanse yourself, or simply sit for five minutes imagining white light burning within and around you, removing all darkness and keeping it at bay.

2. **Create a sacred space for them.** You can do this by cleaning the space you wish to use when contacting them with salt water (to mop the floors and clean any surfaces) or some sage to smudge the area. You can also create an altar by setting up items that you know matter to them on a simple table, before which you'll sit to do your meditation to reach out to your ancestors

3. **Meditate.** Some people like to think of meditation as something it's not. It's simply about maintaining your attention on one thing for an extended time, long enough to allow your conscious mind to relax and access your subconscious and the greater spiritual realm around you. You must find somewhere you won't be bothered for at least ten to fifteen minutes to meditate. Sit or lie down, wearing comfortable clothing, and shut your eyes. Bring your attention to your breath, breathing in through your nose and out through slightly parted lips. After a few breaths, you should start to feel more relaxed in mind and body. Then you can call out to your spirit guides simply by stating you want to be in touch with them or drawing your attention to them in your mind. Meditation should be done daily, not just when you want to reach out to your guides, but as a practice to keep your spiritual senses sharp.

Methods for Getting in Touch with Guides

1. **Make offerings to your ancestors.** When you have set up your altar, you can offer them things you know they'll appreciate. For instance, was there a special kind of clothing they were known to wear? You could put that on the altar. If you know their favorite foods, drinks, and smells, you could also use that. When you've set all the offerings before them, let them know in a short prayer that you're offering these to them to connect with them. Thank them in advance for taking the time and effort to connect with you.

2. **Work with your dreams.** You can connect to your ancestors through your dreams. It's very easy for them to reach out to you through this means. It's not a difficult thing to do. Simply let them know you want to connect with them through your dreams. Set this intention front and center in your mind before you go to bed each night, and they'll eventually show up if they don't during the first night. Also, if you wake up in the middle of the night to pee or something, don't be so quick to open your eyes. Remain in bed and don't move. Relax, and intend to connect with them. You will begin to have visions of them as you lie there or fall back to sleep and dream of them.
3. **Create an anchor.** This is a gesture you make whenever you want to summon your ancestors, but your situation won't allow you to perform your usual cleansing ritual, creating a sacred space for them and meditation. This anchor is best created when you're in the middle of your meditation or prayers to them. For instance, you could try rubbing your right thumb in a clockwise circle over the side of your forefinger as your personal anchor, or you could pinch your elbow or do whatever you want. When you've got an anchor set up, and you need to reach out to your ancestors or other spirit guides in a pinch, simply doing that makes you more aware of their presence, so you can connect with them better.

Keeping the Connection

So, it's not enough to just connect with your ancestors now and then, and it's best to practice this so that they have more power and presence in your life to do things on your behalf. Here are some ways you can keep that line of communication fresh:

1. **Pick a set time of the day or night that you dedicate to communing with them.** You don't have to always ask for things. You could just say hello now and then.
2. **Do you have things you do every day?** You could pick one of those things and decide you're not going to start it without reaching out to them first. It could be anything from brushing your teeth to sitting down to work at your

desk.

3. **Wear something that reminds you of them regularly.** It could be a bracelet, a necklace, or even perfume. Be very intentional about what you choose to remind you of them so that you never forget their significance, and you can keep remembering that you carry them with you wherever you go.

4. **Make a habit of talking to them in your mind.** The more you do this, the more you'll get so comfortable with them that you might even find yourself talking to them aloud. Try not to freak your friends out with this one, so they don't think you're crazy. Conversing with them naturally will make you feel even more at home, opening you up to their love and blessings. Also, you'll notice that they answer you faster and with clearer messages than ever before.

How to Choose the Best Ancestor Guide to Work With

1. **Pick guides that have gained a lot of wisdom from their experiences in life.** This means it's a smart idea to go with the older ancestors, not those who passed away young. The older they are, the more they've experienced in life, which means they have a much better perspective on your life and can let you know what to do by tapping into their vast knowledge. They've had the time and space to make their own mistakes, so they know better. You can take advantage of that. There's no other pool of knowledge you can tap into that will be like theirs. The fact that they've gone past the physical realm into the spiritual realm also means they can combine the new knowledge of their spirit with the old knowledge from the Earth to give you the very best guidance. They can also comfort you convincingly since the odds are they've lived long enough to experience all the highs and lows of life.

2. **Choose the one who has passed away without giving you grief.** Some ancestors are only there to complain about this life or its people, especially younger generations. These spirits require a lot of energy from living family members and often drain them emotionally. That's not to say that our ancestors are joyless, but rather that they realize that problems, hardships, and heartache are part of life, and they don't linger on this topic once they cross over. They respect all living beings on the planet and just want to help those in need, even if it's only a kind word or a little advice.

3. **Choose one that is empathetic.** Everyone has a favorite relative who is helpful and loving without being overly involved. Even though they claim not to have the energy to help, they come through in big ways or small. Such a spirit is more than willing to share their ideas, counsel, and understanding with others at any time. Most people who know about these individuals take note of these details and learn from them when in need. Everyone can use a shoulder to cry on, and a guide who is in touch with their emotions and can empathize with you is the best. Don't go for someone who never cared about you when they were alive. If they didn't while they were here, why would they when they're gone?

4. **Choose the ones who have a positive reputation.** If you're still new to this process, you may want to avoid going for people with a checkered past. Maybe they were troublemakers at some point in their life, and their absence from this world meant fewer problems for your family. Don't work with anyone who wasn't known to be good because they may be bad seeds that want to cause more headaches for you and those who are still alive. Besides, these negative spirits are often very demanding and will not let up until you're a mess. These individuals are draining and have an urge to meddle in every aspect of your life, even when it's none of their business.

5. **Choose the ones you have a common connection with.** Everyone has a spirit guide that they're drawn to, but it's important to remember that blood is not truly thicker than water when it comes to this issue of choosing an ancestral guide who is good for you. You may be more comfortable with someone in your family just because they share your last name, but is that enough? If you can't find anyone in your family or lineage worth working with, it's okay to go with a guide who you know would be good to you, even if they're not a blood relative. If you don't have any other connections, you may as well take those who seem happiest to help. They are there for everyone, regardless of age or background. These spirits are always willing to listen and give their insight on whatever topic. As long as they know you're faithful, they will never turn away from your requests for help.

Chapter Three: Ascended Masters and Historical Figures

All about Ascended Masters

Ascended masters are spirit guides who have ascended, meaning they are no longer held back by the karmic cycle of birth, death, and rebirth. They continue their spiritual evolution in the world of spirits, and from this world, they offer their guidance to those of us still on this cycle to help us ascend just as they have. The lessons these masters have for us here on Earth are of a high, strong vibration, and they must also help you ascend on your path.

Once upon a time, having an ascended master for a guide was reserved only for those souls who were well along their karmic journey, but today, with more light and knowledge, it's easy for those who want to connect with them to do just that. Why would you want an ascended master as your spiritual counsel? Because they've been through everything you're going through, and they've learned to overcome it all, which means they can show you how.

When you're ready to wake up from the dream of physical reality, access your Christ consciousness and move on to the next level spiritually, your ascended masters will show up for you. There are many ascended masters available, but remember that not all of them choose to teach. The ones meant to cross paths with you are a perfect fit for your unique life and experiences, which is why working with them is the best thing you can do for yourself.

Stories about Meeting Ascended Masters

This is Layla's story: *"Here's what happened when I met my ascended master, who told me I could call him Mariel. My ascended master came to me in a dream, during a time when I had decided that I would be more dedicated to my spiritual walk. I never dreamed of having one, so I was very surprised to find that I did. He explained that he had been assigned as my guide for my whole life and would continue to be with me on my spiritual path until the end. He told me that he'd come at this time to help guide me on my journey out of my body and into the light. He described his role as being to help me overcome any barriers I may have had that prevented me from taking the next step toward enlightenment."*

Here's an account by Starr about how she got experienced her meeting with her ascended master when she was just a young girl: *"When I was a young girl, I had a very stern, gentle teacher. He taught me how to breathe and hold my body in a way that strengthened me and prepared me for life. He appeared to me many times, usually in the company of my mother or grandmother, who were both deceased. He would appear when I was alone and wanted to know something he happened to want to teach me. I would always sit in a chair, and he would appear before me. He was a tall, thin man with long black hair, piercing blue eyes, and surrounded by a white halo that surrounded him like misty clouds. With time, he would appear to be alone, as I no longer needed my grandma or mom to assure me that my experiences were real and safe."*

How to Connect to Your Ascended Master Guide

One thing you must remember about ascended masters is that they're non-conditional. In other words, they won't place any requirements on you when working with you. They understand the importance of free will and will honor yours. In other words, you will not get any intervention unless and until you ask them for help. Before attempting to connect with them, please make sure you use the preparation methods from the previous chapter to be ready and safe. Now, let's talk about how you can reach out to them.

Say a simple prayer. Your prayers don't have to be complicated. You can just say "thank you" to them, whether for something good you've experienced or something you'd like them to do on your behalf. A prayer of thanks is more than enough to connect with them, as thankfulness is a state of being that is pretty high in vibration. Make sure you feel the appreciation coming from within you as you thank them for their love, guidance, support, protection, provision, and all else you want to express.

Meditate on their picture. If you know your ascended master, you can meditate on an image of them if you've got one. This is actually the best way to do it if you're a beginner because you're already connected to these people through emotions. You will feel more sensation when doing this - which is a good thing. As a bonus, if you happen to be working with a group of ascended masters, looking at their pictures during meditation will help you distinguish their individual energies one from one another. You can ask for the different masters' help in specific situations or their guidance about life. Don't know what they look like? Check out the next suggestion.

Meditating on your ascended master guide's image can help you connect with them.
https://unsplash.com/photos/HS5CLnQbCOc?utm_source=unsplash&utm_medium=re ferral&utm_content=creditShareLink

Connect with them in your dreams. Before you go to bed, intend to meet them in your dreams. They will show up as long as you continue to make that intention clear, and you keep an open mind to them. It's helpful to thank them as if they've already made themselves known to you in your dreams because that will make them show up faster.

Notice the signs you get in your physical reality. To help you understand just what this means, here's an experience that Jesse had: *"Just as I was sitting here in my chair, writing this, I noticed a door in my house open and shut all by itself. This isn't the first time it's occurred, and it's not like it's a faulty door or anything of the sort. So, what's going on? I know my ascended master is here with me, and looking at the time, I can tell that it's exactly one minute until to when I should be meditating. This tends to happen simultaneously, like clockwork, and I know it's no coincidence because I had a dream where I saw my ascended master open and shut a door and then tell me to note the time. Since that dream, they've always used that medium to remind me when it's time to do some spiritual work."* What strange things are happening around you? Start paying close attention.

Channel the masters through writing. This is another way to connect with them, and it can be done in an internal dialogue or journal. When you're in a quiet place, ask them for help. Then write down what they say to you as soon as possible after you get the information you seek. In other words, don't worry about how silly it may sound out loud – just do it. Flow with it. Trust is essential if you're going to get anything that's worth something from them. If nothing shows up immediately, just know it will after some time. If you can no longer hear anything in your mind, or the thought impressions they send you stop coming through, read out loud what you've written so far, and add more things to it on your own about what you've learned from what they shared.

Connect with the masters through painting. This is another type of art-based channeling where you release your creative spirit in the process. Pick up a paintbrush and draw whatever you feel guided to draw by the ascended masters. You will immediately feel their presence and be able to communicate with them. If you can't figure out what to draw, close your eyes and ask the ascended master for help again. As with any other type of channeling, you can also release what you've drawn into the universe so that it may be used in a way that's good for everyone or to manifest a specific intent you may have.

Keeping the Connection to Your Ascended Master Guide

1. **Learn how to lucid dream.** Connecting with these guides is easier when you have better control of your dreams.
2. **Learn how to astral project.** Astral projection will help when they need to show you things on the other side of the planet or a different universe entirely, rather than working with you through your subjective dreams.
3. **Meditate often.** When you meditate, you will inevitably become more sensitive to their energies, making them reach out to you with any information they feel you need to know, which will benefit your life tremendously.

Historical Figure Guides

Historical spirit guides are exactly what they sound like. These are historical figures who once lived on Earth and are no more. You can work with them as guides too if you want to. Suppose you notice that you're particularly drawn to a certain historical figure. In that case, the odds are that you will find it easy to connect with them if you want to.

Before you connect with a historical figure, you need to do your homework to know all there is to know about them. You should look into where they were born and raised, what they were known for, what it was like living with them, what they liked and disliked, and anything else you can learn about them. Looking for the perfect historical figure guide for you is to consider where you're at in life right now and then think about the sort of energy that could help you along your journey as you research different figures. You'll have no trouble knowing when you've spotted the right guide for you as you do this.

Here's how Dmitri connected with Mozart as a spirit guide. "*I was desperately seeking motivation, and for a long time, making music no longer gave me the same joy it used to. When I learned I could work with great musicians who had passed on as guides, I was beyond ecstatic. I chose to work with Mozart as I'd always loved his sound and originality. Since then, I've had no regrets. He's helped me find my spark again, and now my music has added dimensions and quality to it that I never in my wildest dreams thought I could achieve.*"

How to Connect with Your Historical Figure Guide

As always, please remember to practice safety first. Prepare your body, mind, and space for connecting with these guides before you get into it.

Figure out who you want to work with. As you learn about great people who did amazing things in different aspects of life, think about how your life could parallel theirs and check in with your heart to see who calls out to you. You'll know who it is because their name will either jump out at you, you may dream about them, or you'll stumble across information that confirms they're the ones you should be working with through synchronistic events like seeing an article on them, or hearing about them.

Use items they would always carry as totems to draw their energy. For instance, if a figure you've chosen always had a pipe with them, you could buy one and keep it in their honor or place it on your altar when you want to connect with them.

Meditate on their essence. Simply relax during your meditation, and then bring their names to your mind. You can also conjure up a picture of them in your mind and then sense their energy enveloping you fully as you meditate on them.

Work with them in dreams. The beautiful thing about dreams is that they make it easy for you to connect with those who have passed on, no matter how long ago they died. So set an intention before you go to sleep that you'd like to connect with them. If you have a question for them, fix that question in your mind, and quietly affirm your thankfulness to them in advance for showing up and giving you the answer you seek.

Visit historical sites connected to them. When you go to these sites, you should get a sense of their energy and be able to connect to them deliberately. You'll find it's smart to look into the historical figures in your own hometown, as it means you'll have easy access to their old homes or favorite locations that they were known to visit often. You're likely to leave an energetic imprint when you often go or live somewhere. So, going to these places will make it easy for you to connect with your guides. With time, you may not need to make these visits as they become more familiar to you, which means you can work with them whenever and wherever you want.

Chapter Four: Elemental Beings and Nature Spirits

Elementals and nature beings aren't human in any way, though they can actually take on the form of humans if they want to. They are the spiritual essence of the natural elements and the rest of nature. Let's begin by discussing elementals.

Elemental Beings

There are four types of this kind of being, and each is connected to one of the four classical elements; Earth, fire, air, and water. Gnomes are considered earth elementals. Salamanders and sylphs are fire and air elementals, respectively. Mermaids are water elementals. It's important to note that there's a fifth element known as ether, akasha, or spirit, which we as humans possess. You should know how elements affect us if you work with elemental beings as guides.

When you're working with water, you'll be much better at feeling your emotions, expressing them, and being a loving person. When you're working with air, you're more in touch with your creative side, able to create wonderful art and find the beauty in all things. When you work with the earth, you want to deal with grounded matters and create a world where things last and have value. When you work with fire, it's all about power and will. It's a very expansive element, and its sheer intensity makes it possible for you to deal with anything that keeps you from being your authentic self to the fullest.

The following is Venus's account of how she connected with an elemental being names Gaia: "After learning about her, meditating on her energy signature, and then going to sleep with her on my mind, I dreamed of a tall woman who was like a nature goddess and who looked like she was very wise. She said to me, '*You're doing just fine on your journey.*' She gave me the information that I needed. She then said that I should align myself with the four elements to find balance and harmony in life. She also permitted me to ask her in the future if I need help with any of my other elemental guides."

Signs an Elemental Is Calling to You

1. **You keep having dreams about their element.** If you're always dreaming of water, fire, earth, or air, there's a chance that's because you have a special connection to the spirits of these elements. They could inspire you to take concrete action toward reaching out and developing a mutually beneficial relationship with them.

2. **You feel like you're undergoing an awakening.** There's a reason why many people experience physical symptoms when their elemental being is calling out to them. While it's not guaranteed every time, it's worth paying attention to your body and feeling what is happening to it as you become more aware of your internal energy in relation to the surrounding elements.

3. **You start to become obsessed with the element.** If you are outside; it's a stormy day. The lightning is making your hair stand on end, or you're in the shower thinking about water as hard as you can. Strange things start happening around you; this is a sign your elemental guide is trying to communicate with you. You may also experience intense physiological phenomena, such as an increased heart rate or vision alteration.

4. **Strange visions are assailing you.** In dreams, people's elemental guides can be as varied as those they guide. Some dreams they show me are more animalistic and

feral, while others are more ethereal and spiritual. Just remember that it is your elemental spirit guides you are seeing, not something else in the dream world. If you feel someone is trying to penetrate your subconscious mind or consciousness deeply through dreams and visions, this is a sign that the spirit wants to speak with you somehow.

5. **You feel energy signatures or bursts of overwhelming sensations.** Some people experience a rush of energy near certain geographic locations that resonate with different elements. For example, if you're walking along the beach in Santa Monica, and it's a beautiful sunny day, you might feel like your heart is being pulled toward the ocean. If this always happens, this may be a sign from your spirit that the element of water is calling to you.

How to Connect with Your Elemental Spirit Guide

1. **Ask your elemental guide to contact you.** You can ask your elemental guide to contact you in any way. You can call out to the elements, for example, through prayer or writing a letter summoning them to you.
2. **Trust that they will come.** Your spirit guides won't show up until they know they're trusted and will be welcomed by you. They may offer you a message when you're ready for them to. These messages can profoundly affect your life and the world around you.
3. **Examine your dreams.** If you have dreams about spirits or entities, pay attention to the element being called to you. You may dream of the nature of these spirits, where they call from, their appearance and traits and qualities, and even their purpose for contacting you.
4. **Listen to your body.** Just as the Earth speaks to you, your body will often speak to you in energy sensations. Listen to what it has to say.
5. **Get out in nature.** Being away from the city and going into nature can be a great way to connect with your spiritual side. And, when you do get outside, seek out the element

calling you the loudest.

Being around nature is one of the ways to connect with your spiritual side.
https://unsplash.com/photos/ndN00KmbJ1c?utm_source=unsplash&utm_medium=referral&utm_content=creditShareLink

6. **Meditate in nature.** I truly believe there's no better place on Earth than the vast landscapes of planet Earth, especially when they're wild and untamed. One of my favorite things is meditating in the mountains after a long day of hiking or camping. By reaching out with your energy to the elements and the Earth, you open up the energy coursing through our planet.

7. **Say prayers to the elementals.** You can always pray if you aren't comfortable meditating or writing to your elemental spirit guides. Praying is a way to express your desire to communicate with them. Your prayer doesn't have to be fancy or formal. It's literally just a conversation with the elementals, telling them what you want to and listening out for them to see if you get any answers on the inside or in your physical world through synchronicity and signs.

Honoring Your Elemental Beings

1. **Leave them gifts in nature.** Just as you leave gifts on the altar for your gods, you can offer things to your elemental guides as a sign of gratitude. These may be special items such as traditional foods that are special to the element they are associated with, or natural and handmade items made by local artists and craftspeople.
2. **Observe nature.** Being in nature can offer many opportunities to connect with the elements, from being out in the woods, trekking through a mountain, or being at a beach.
3. **Perform ceremonies.** There are many ways to honor the elements, from small handmade offerings to rituals in nature and celebrations of traditions such as Celtic fire rites.
4. **Greet your spirit guides.** Do this with respect and love. Remember that you're talking to your fellow travelers on this journey through life, and make an effort to be friendly and knowledgeable about who these elements are.

What Are Nature Spirits?

Nature spirits are non-physical entities that live in and around nature. They exist in their own realm and have the trust of the elements. Many people confuse nature spirits with elementals, but there are differences. Elementals are spirits that come from the elements. Nature spirits are part of the elementals, either as helpers or a conglomeration of other elements, depending on their role in spirit work and helping humans. They are made of etheric matter, and they help to sculpt reality.

Here's how Darren connected with a nature spirit in a tree in his backyard: *"I had been working on connecting with spirits in my life. I kept getting this strange feeling each time I saw the image of the apple tree from my backyard in my mind repeatedly. So, one day I decided to go into my backyard and greet it, and that's when it happened. I felt this strange energy come over me. It was as if I was talking to an old friend I hadn't seen for a long time.*

The energy was very welcoming. Whatever it was, it asked me if I wanted to work with it, and I accepted. Ever since then, I've been doing that tree's will and working with nature spirits in general."

Riley found a deep connection with the spirit of their local pond. Here's their story: *"I first felt drawn to the pond over a year ago and have come back several times since then, always trying to get a better feel for the spirits in this place. I've meditated a few times here and found that their energy is strong. The last time I was here, I brought some of my friends, and we all felt the presence of something spiritual. But, with so many people, it was hard to know what was what. Nature spirits are not used to large crowds and may have sensed us as more of a threat than anything else.*

"I'd been thinking about this pond for a few days when I finally decided to come here again by myself and with my journal in my hand. I felt a strong urge to sit down on the bank of the pond and write and meditate. My eyes scanned the surface, and I saw something in the distance. The closer I looked, the clearer it became that it was a swan, and it didn't appear to be swimming at all. It was moving flawlessly through the water with its head held high toward the bank where I was sitting.

"Then, I saw something else. The swan had another being with it, and this other being was coming up near the surface of the water toward me. This creature's head was also held high, and it seemed to be looking at me. I wanted to see its face, but as it came closer, there was some kind of mist that blocked my view. I got a message, like a block of thought in my head, about how it was a nature spirit. I right away got into my meditation and connected with it. The lessons I learned from it changed my life forever."

Signs a Nature Spirit Is Calling to You

1. **You get a feeling of warmth around you when you're outside in nature.** In addition to warmth, some people feel a sense of fellowship and acceptance from nature spirits. Others feel as though they are literally surrounded by the element they want to meet.

2. **You will see signs in nature.** The natural world is the unique way that nature spirits communicate with humans. They may appear as a rainbow, their symbol, or as a beautiful animal or plant.
3. **You feel a sense of peace, love, and harmony.** Nature spirits are very interested in helping humanity, especially the planet Earth, which is all about growth and evolution.
4. **You have visions or nightmares about nature.** Some people say that nature spirits influence their dreams. Some people even claim to have had experiences where they saw the actual beings of nature around them as if they were real. Others speak of a spirit guide who comes to them in their dreams and gives them directions via the dream world.
5. **You smell a plant or flower that isn't around you.** Some people report being able to smell nature even when they're not out in it. Some smell plants, while others report smelling animals like squirrels or birds.

How to Connect with Your Nature Spirit Guide

After preparing your mind, space, and body to connect with these guides, you can proceed with getting in touch with them.

1. **Pray to your spirit guide.** You can ask the spirits anything you want to. In the woods, you can lie down in a place of worship and say prayers to them. Again, praying is simply telling them anything you want to. You can ask for the spirit of a tree or any other nature to lend you a hand in your life. It can be an amazing experience, especially if you already have a relationship with that nature spirit.
2. **Ask them specific questions.** Some people believe that nature spirits are good listeners and will answer their questions. Other people say that not all nature spirits know everything. Either way, it's a good idea to be prepared with a few questions with answers that have always eluded you because these beings are wise and willing to help you all the time.

3. **Get out in the woods or other natural environments.** If you want to connect with your local nature spirits, this is the best thing you can do. Getting out in wooded areas, areas with water and sand, or where you can build a fire, and studying nature, will bring you closer together with these spirits.
4. **Have a feast in their honor:** Some people believe feasts to nature spirits are a great way to bring you closer to them. They may ask for a small offering or simply want you to enjoy the food and drink in honor of them.
5. **Meditate.** This is another method of connecting with nature spirits of the woods and other areas for those who can't get out into the natural world because life gets in the way sometimes.

Honoring Your Nature Spirit Guides

1. **Become a vegetarian.** Many nature spirits are vegetables or animals, so becoming a vegetarian is a powerful way to honor them.
2. **Drink tea.** Some people believe that by drinking natural, herbal teas, you can gain the powers of the nature spirits of those plants.
3. **Wear crystals.** Going out into the wilderness, it's a great idea to wear crystals on your body to attract nature spirits and create harmony with them for any other purpose you might have in mind.

Chapter Five: Working with Spirit Animals

Spirit animals are perhaps the most well-known type of spirit guides. But what is a spirit animal? According to Native American legend, a spirit animal guides its human counterpart as they navigate through life by showing them their strengths and weaknesses. Certain animals are known to have this effect on some people more than others. For example, some people may associate with a wolf, while others may see a bat as a sign of protection.

The idea of spirit animals is not new and has been around for centuries — but the list of spirit animals is constantly changing along with modern culture and beliefs. When looking for the answer to the question of whether your spirit animal is real, you must understand that we are all blessed with a spirit animal. The signs they give us allow us to learn when to expect changes in our lives and give us a key to understanding certain situations surrounding us. Without proper guidance from your spirit animal, you may be in some type of misfortune or even make mistakes. Your spirit animal is always there for you and will never leave you.

Whether you realize it or not, your spirit animal may affect several aspects of your life. It is important to know that your guides are always there for you, and it is up to you to acknowledge their presence in your life. Your spirit animal can be an excellent source of strength, happiness, and insight whenever you need them the most.

The great thing about spirit animals is that they are supposed to help you, not hinder you. They are always with you and will guide you along your path. However, to keep them happy, you must be respectful to them and learn how to listen to their advice. They will often be happy and helpful and guide you along the right path if you show respect. Obey their advice, and your life will be filled with both happiness and insight.

Let Oliver share how he learned about his spirit animal and reached out to it: "I was looking for an animal spirit to work with, but I didn't have anyone in mind. So, I asked my spirit guides for help. They told me about the animal best suited for me, and it was a bear. I believe this animal spirit chose me as his guide and has been with me every step of the way. I started out by making my ancestor's totem pictures and placing them in my home." Oliver already had some experience working with his guides, so it was easy for him to ask them for help, and they came through. You can do the same thing, too.

Karen has a story about how she found her own spirit animal. Here it is: *"Here's how I connected with my spirit animal. I was in a car with my family driving home when I decided to take a moment to reflect on my life. I was riding in the backseat, staring out the window, and feeling self-conscious about how depressing it had all become with how each day could easily be described as an exhausting battle of constant struggles. It seemed like all it would take for me to reach hopelessness was one more thing going wrong. So, I asked the universe, "Is there anything you can do to make my life better?" I then got a very unexpected answer in my heart; "Connect with your spirit animal." I wanted to know what it was, and right then, I saw a big billboard with a swan on it. I just knew right then and there. My spirit animal was a swan. Ever since I began working with the swan, so many miraculous, marvelous things have happened in my life."*

Naomi discovered her spirit animal was a lion. Here's how: *"Here's how I discovered the lion is my spirit animal. I always thought I was a cat person, but one day as I was daydreaming in class, on the brink of sleep, I realized I would rather be a lion.*

I always wanted to be in the limelight, doing something great and special. But the dreaded voice in my head kept telling me that I would fail, that I wasn't good enough to do these things. Then I fell asleep briefly, and there was a vivid flash of a beautiful lion standing before me gracefully and powerfully. It said to me, "I'm with you. You will find success in all you do if you work with me now and always." I wasn't a spiritual person before, but after that day, I chose to look into spirit animals and began working with my lion's energy. I have had no regrets since then."

Spirit Animals, Totem Animals, and Power Animals

Where your spirit animal is a guide, your totem animal is your essence. It's your energy or who you really are. Your power animal is the energy you draw upon from the spirit realm when you need strength or help with something in your life. You can ask this power to remain active all through your life or only to be activated when you're in trouble or need to help someone else.

Signs Your Spirit Animal Is Calling to You

1. **You have dreams where you see them all the time.** Dreams can be very useful to help you learn about your spirit animal. For instance, if you have loads of dreams where an animal is chasing you, it may not necessarily be a nightmare. It could signify that your spirit animal wants to get your attention.

2. **You see them in your everyday life.** If you see your spirit animal during your day-to-day activities, it's a sign that they're around and watching over you. If you see an animal out of the corner of your eye, and it disappears, this could also mean that your spirit animal is trying to get you to notice them.

3. **You hear them even when they're not around.** People have reported hearing their spirit animal's sounds without any animals being around or right in their ears just before going to bed or waking up. You may experience this yourself when you start connecting with them actively.

4. **You feel them**. Suppose you feel as though something with primal, animalistic energy is watching over you. In that case, it might be a signal from your spirit animal. It might be difficult to recognize at first if they're nearby, but once you do, listen carefully because they'll start talking to you differently.
5. **You sense a shift in your life.** Have you felt an overwhelming urge to take action in some area of your life, powered by primal instincts? It could signify that your spirit animal shows you the best path to take.

Can You Have More Than One Spirit Animal?

Even though it seems like it would be difficult to have more than one spirit animal, the answer is yes. Although this may seem strange, people have been known to have several spirit animals in their lives. It can help you know that you have more than one support system in life, and you don't have to be alone.

Some people may have one as a "primary" spirit animal and others as the secondary one. This can depend on various factors, such as your needs at the time. For instance, if you are having trouble with someone in your life, you may be guided by a spirit animal specializing in protection and defense. This is just one example, but you could find that a variety of spirit animals guide you during your lifetime in different situations. It's all about finding the one that best suits you at the time and in whatever situation you happen to be in.

It's also important to be aware that having multiple spirit animals doesn't mean that they are supposed to make their presence known equally. Some may show up more than others because this is required at a certain time in your life. So, not every spirit animal you have needs to show up often. Some people's lives may be easier than others, which may mean that the nature of your spirit animals will vary.

A spirit animal is a spiritual guide you come into contact with and then bond with them, or you can be born with them. They are like guardian angels who have watched over us since we were kids.

They can be described as a higher intelligence within us, and they can help us in case we need some guidance.

How to Find Your Spirit Animal

1. **Use your intuition.** The best way to determine your spirit animal is to use your intuition. You can feel them when they are around, and you will know the exact moment they are there, which can be really helpful. If you feel that a particular animal is the one you need to be with, it can be very helpful to speak to them. I suggest you try and get in touch with them if you are having any major problems in your life, so they can help guide you.

2. **Try meditation.** Another way to figure out your spirit animal is by going on a meditation retreat. Wherever you are, your spirit animal will make itself known to you. You mustn't overexert yourself when meditating because this can cause the spirit animal to leave once again or not even show up. When meditating, it's good to breathe in the scent of any nearby animals and then picture them in your mind. This opens up the communication process that helps meet your spiritual companion.

3. **Take a walk in nature.** Going for a walk in the wild can be incredibly helpful if you are feeling lost and confused about what to do. Getting out of the city and into nature can help you feel more at peace with yourself, and this can make your spirit animal physically or spiritually come forward to help you. You may find they will speak out loud when they are around, or they may just give you a sign that lets you know they are there.

4. **Do a reading.** You can also do readings to figure out your spirit animal. There are variations of doing a reading that can help you determine what your spirit animal is. A lot of native cultures will use methods like this. Some psychics will just know what your spirit animals are without even having to do any sort of ritual.

5. **Connect with your elders.** Another way you can learn about your spirit animal is by talking to the elders in your family or community. They may be able to hint at what it

is, or they may even tell you that they know exactly what it is. If they don't, I suggest trying the other techniques before speaking with them again.

How to Connect to Your Spirit Animal

1. **Visualize them.** A good way to connect with your spirit animal is by visualizing them. This can be done through meditation or just thinking about them from time to time. If you want to know yourself better, then I suggest you try this technique, as it helps open up communication with the spiritual side of yourself.

2. **Ask for signs.** When you feel your spirit animal is close by, do what you can to find out their name and what they represent. This can be done in two ways: thinking about them and asking for a name to pop into your head or asking them to appear in front of you somehow and ask for their name.

3. **Learn about their characteristics.** What do spirit animals represent? Each animal has their own unique characteristics. Learning what they represent can help you connect to them more easily.

4. **Talk to your spirit animal.** Sometimes, our spirit animals can help us out in times of need, and they are capable of offering advice as well. This can be done through meditation or thinking about them when you need help.

5. **Ask them for help.** If you are ever in need of guidance, then I suggest you call out to your spirit animal. They can help you when you are in a jam, but they will only come if they think it is necessary. You should also write down what you need help with and then burn that piece of paper. This can help clear the path to communication between the two of you, and it will make it easier for your spirit animal to talk back to you.

6. **Don't force the connection.** Quite often, people will try to forcefully connect to their spirit animal to get proof that they exist. This is not the best way to go about it, as it can make your spirit animal leave you, or it can make them

become more hidden from you.
7. **Have faith.** That is important if you have faith in your spiritual companion and know they are there. They will eventually make themselves known to you, and if they are not in your life yet, then don't worry. They will show up when the time is right.
8. **Ask your spirit guides to show you your spirit animal.** Your spirit guides will know which animals you're supposed to connect and work with.

How to Honor Your Spirit Animal

You must show some respect and honor your spirit animal in much the same way you care about the well-being of physical animals on earth. These spirit animals have been assigned to take care of you and deserve to be shown some appreciation. It only makes sense to honor them and treat them as more than just helpers and messengers. Doing this will create a powerful bond between you, and they will be able to serve you better in turn because of your devotion to them.

Many people choose to name their spirit animals and tattoo them on their person. This practice comes from Native American cultures and has been adopted by many groups, including African American heritage and spiritual practitioners like Celts, Druids, Ancient Egyptians, etc. Here are other ways you can honor your spirit animal.

1. **Make offerings to your spirit animal.** You can honor your spirit animal by offering them and putting them in a place where you will see them. Offerings can be anything from food to clothing and more.
2. **Connect with them just to say hello.** I would suggest using meditation or just thinking about your spirit animal occasionally. Your spirit animal is there for a reason, so honoring them is necessary if you want them to stick around. You shouldn't wait until you need help to reach out.

3. **Consult your elders.** Your elders may have some information on how to go about honoring your spirit animal better. Talk to them and see what they have to say. They are often very knowledgeable about finding our animal guides and other spiritual beings.
4. **Wear jewelry that reminds you of their presence.** Make it something unique that reminds you of the animal alone.

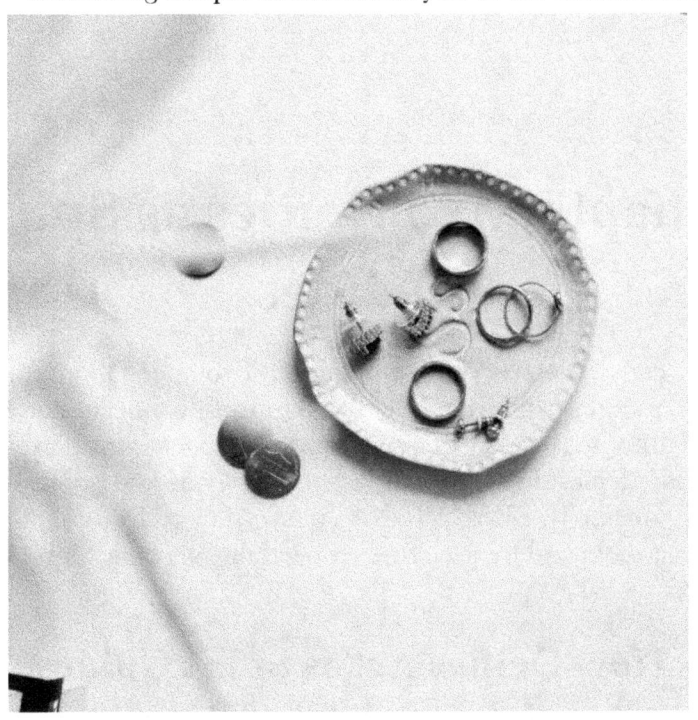

Honor your spirit animal by wearing jewelry that reminds you of their presence.
https://unsplash.com/photos/ECr_8nuXpBA?utm_source=unsplash&utm_medium=referral&utm_content=creditShareLink

Chapter Six: Deities as Spirit Guides

Deities can also act as your spirit guides if you need them to. It's a matter of finding out which deity you're most connected or drawn to and then making it your mission to connect with them. Who are these deities, to begin with? They are gods and goddesses. It doesn't matter which religion or culture they're from; as long as you treat them and their culture respectfully, it's okay to work with them.

How Deities Act as Spirit Guides

Deities may not always offer you direct help, but they can point your guardian angel toward the right course of action for you, and your guardian angel can, in turn, communicate that to you. It's important to note that deities aren't a permanent part of your spiritual army of guides. They'll show up and help but then be on their way. More often than not, when you call on them, they will send you a message or the answer you seek through some other spirit guide.

The thing to note about gods and goddesses as guides is that they can help you whenever you want, but often, *it's just easier to work with your other spirit guides.* This isn't because the deities can't or won't help you, but because they're more inclined to intervene personally when you're in particularly dire straits. You can turn to many deities, like Amadioha, Horus, Kali, Selene, the Buddha, and more. You just need to do your homework to figure out which of them you resonate with the most.

Nikita shared her story about connecting with the goddess Luna as a spirit guide: *"I've always been a huge fan of the moon, and when I realized how connected it is to everyone, I decided to focus on her and see what would happen next. It started with just me noticing a lot of synchronicities surrounding the moon. Then, I began seeing the goddess's face framed by the moon in my dreams, but I wasn't sure if that was just a coincidence or not. Then, one day when I was meditating, I noticed that she was speaking to me. She was saying, 'You are always connected to the moon. It is part of who you are.' I don't see her often and only choose to work with her when I have a very troublesome situation. She's lovely to work with and has unmistakable power."*

Signs a Deity Is Around You

1. **You notice a lot more synchronicity in your life.** You realize that the universe has been conspiring to work with you and not against you, and this causes a sense of empowerment in you. You notice way more happy little "coincidences" that are a little too perfect for you to think of as just random events in your life.

2. **You feel more positive and uplifted.** You realize that you're surrounded by love, and it feels good. Your moods are more positive, you smile more, and the world just feels like a better place to be because of all the love you feel. You know that higher powers are here to support you, making you want to be a kinder, more compassionate person.

3. **You hear unusual noises or voices that others can't understand.** The voices are usually soothing and gentle, but they don't always make sense to you at first. This is because they sometimes come to you in other forms - like sounds or images - instead of words. Usually, you'll experience these phenomena in deep meditation or when you're on the cusp of sleep and being awake.

4. **The spirit world becomes more accessible to you.** Deities can help you get in touch with your guardian angels if you're curious about what they have to say, and it's easier for your other guides and angels to help you in general. They can make you more aware of the world beyond the veil.
5. **You start to experience spiritual gifts.** You may suddenly find that the things you say tend to come to pass or that you have visions or flashes of the future. You could develop Clairaudience, Claircognizance, Clairsentience, Clairvoyance, or Clairgustance. You may notice you can pick on what people are feeling and thinking more or that your desires are starting to manifest at what feels like warp speed. All of these result from the intense energies of the deities around you, who naturally lend their power to yours to make you a little more than human.

Which Deity Should You Choose?

To figure this out, you must expose yourself to as many deities as possible while checking in with your gut to see which one pulls at you. Some people just know right off the bat; for others, it will take more time and research. Either way works.

Another way you can discover which deity you should be working with is to look at your ancestry, trace as far back as you can, and see who exactly your ancestors used to worship when they were still alive. You could then make that god or goddess your go-to spirit guide for when you need that extra spiritual muscle to back you up.

If you can't trace your lineage for some reason, it's not a bad idea to check in with a professional, genuine psychic. The psychic will be able to read your energy, note any other god-like energies that are attached to you or that you resonate with, and give you an answer about who you should work with. Don't be shocked if they can't figure it out on the first visit, though. It may take some time.

You could also use a pendulum to help you discover which deity to work with. Get a pendulum from any new age store or an online store. Next, write out the names of every deity of interest to you. Figure out which way your pendulum swings for yes and no by asking yourself questions to which you already know the answers and noting how the pendulum swings in response. When you know which swing is yes and which is no, allow the pendulum to swing over each name on your list, and then note the response you get. Trust that that's the deity you should work with as a guide.

Another thing about deities is that each has specific symbols and correspondences. For instance, if you're drawn to Hecate, you should know that her symbols include crossroads, keys, torches, dogs, and the triple moon. So, if you've seen these symbols around you, the odds are that's the goddess to work with. The same applies to all other deities. Also, consider that if the god or goddess in question is calling you to work with you or responding to your request to work with them, you might notice their symbols tend to show up more often than usual in your life. This is a sign that you're good with them, and they are with you.

Remember that it's a good idea to make offerings to your deity. Some deity guides will require more rituals and offerings than others to provide you with whatever you seek, so when you're doing your homework on deities, you should also keep this in mind so that it's easy to appease them.

How to Connect with Your Deity Spirit Guide

Remember what you need to do before you attempt to connect with your deity. You should cleanse your body with salt water and/or sage, cleanse your space, and clear your mind with meditation before you begin to reach out to them. All this will keep you safe and help foster a deeper connection between you and your chosen deity.

1. **Meditate on them**. Once you've decided which deity you want to work on connecting with, meditate. Once you're deep in meditation, you'll feel a shift happening inside of you. Don't be surprised if your deity begins to address you directly through blocks of thought. They may also present an image to you or create a distinct sound that you perceive within you, which has a very observable effect on your body and mind.

2. **Visualize yourself sitting with your deity and having a conversation.** Imagine they're right there with you, and let them know what it is you'd like them to help you with, trusting that they will deliver the answers you seek. This works especially well when you're trying to get guidance on something that's troubling you.
3. **Put something sacred belonging to your deity in a place of honor.** If you can, get something that belongs to your deities, like a statue or a painting. Place it somewhere in the room where you spend most of your time so that the visual reminder helps you regularly connect with your spirit guide. The object could also be an heirloom that you inherit from your family. There are plenty of things to choose from because deities are connected to virtually every culture on this planet.
4. **Pray.** Prayer is a powerful way to connect with your deity when you don't know what else to do. Praying will help you feel better and happier, which is the entire point of connecting more with the spiritual realm.
5. **Work with them in your dreams.** If you use either lucid dreaming or astral travel, try focusing on your deity while you're dreaming. This creates a very powerful connection to them on a spiritual level.
6. **Use charms, talismans, and other objects with meaning to you.** If there's something that's particularly meaningful to you connected to your deities, like a pendant or even just a little rock with a nice shape or aesthetic quality to it, see if it helps you connect with your spirit guide.
7. **Make offerings and perform rituals.** This is especially powerful if you have a deity you've been worshiping for a long time and feel indebted to them. A ritual offering can be as simple as lighting a candle in their name or as complex as an entire ceremony. The offering is what binds the connection between the two of you, so don't let it go to waste. This offering is payment for all the good that they do for you in your life.

Performing rituals can help you connect with your deity.
https://unsplash.com/photos/x5hyhMBjR3M?utm_source=unsplash&utm_medium=referral&utm_content=creditShareLink

Ritual to Reach Out to Any Deity You Desire

1. Sit in the center of the room you usually spend time in.
2. Light a candle, preferably one used for a ritual for the deity you're trying to connect with. You can also use incense if you have it or just play some music.
3. Perform your first intention. As you begin, glance up at the image of your deity and ask them to help you with whatever it is you want to know from them.
4. Perform your second intention. Then, after you've finished meditating, take the time to thank them for being there with you, and ask them to help you in any way they can.
5. Take the time to truly enjoy the feeling of your deity being present within you. It may be a subtle feeling, but they are always there if you just begin listening for them.
6. Make an offering to them in exchange for their service. For example, you could offer her dirt from a crossroads or a key in Hecate's case.

When it comes to the intention you set for your rituals, you must ensure you're certain about what you want. Words are very powerful, and the deities will hear anything you wish them to, so if you wish for something that's not pure of heart, they may take that as a command and act on it unexpectedly.

Honoring Your Deity Spirit Guide to Maintain the Connection

1. **Always remember them.** This is the most important part. Don't let your connection with them fade because you don't see a direct benefit to it in your life. They're there with you in spirit and want to work with you as much as you want to work with them.
2. **Use the gifts they give you.** When they give you something like a dream or a message, take advantage of that gift by learning from it and applying it to your life in any way that feels right for you. If you gave a friend gifts and they never opened or used them, odds are you'd be upset and quit giving them anything. It's the same principle here. Make a point of using the gifts you're given.
3. **Write them a thank-you note.** Regularly writing down the things that you're grateful for and thanking your deity works wonders for this connection because, even though it's not a direct connection, it creates the mindset that you'd like to maintain a good relationship with them and not take them for granted.
4. **Worship them in your mind.** We all know that the mind is an important part of the spiritual experience. Take the time to imagine what it would be like to have a relationship with your deity and form a gist of their personality and preferences. This will help you see where you could work on improving your connection with them.
5. **Keep photos of them where you can see them and be reminded of them.** Sure, this might be considered a little more "new age" and not everyone's cup of tea, but if you have a picture of your deity or some sort of physical representation of them in your home, this is a great way to

keep them in your life even if they're not physically around you.

6. **Make offerings and sacrifices.** Sacrifice is an important part of any relationship with a deity - unless you're the type who doesn't like to be indebted to anyone else. Suppose you've done something that displeases your deity. In that case, you can make an offering to them in your mind, or even if you have done something that they are proud of, you can make an offering to them so they know how happy they made you.

7. **Dedicate a space in your home for them.** This is the most important thing you can do to connect strongly with your deity. Take the time to set up a spot in your house or apartment where you can do this. It doesn't have to be anything special, but it should be somewhere they can watch over you as you go about your day and involve something that feels familiar to them - maybe a small statue or something along those lines.

Be patient and persistent. The path of spiritual learning is a long and winding one. Just because you can't regularly connect right now doesn't mean it will not happen. Keep at it, and don't give up. You'll eventually find your groove.

Chapter Seven: Understanding Angels and Archangels

Angels and archangels can be very helpful spiritual allies, and you're about to find out just how you can work with them in this chapter. Certain spiritual beings have very high vibrations, working only with the energies of truth, love, and appreciation. They're not held back by anything that keeps us restricted in the physical world, and they have various assignments and purposes in our lives. Whenever you get mired in low-vibration emotions like hate, fear, anger, and so on, you can turn to these guides to help you feel more like your authentic self once more. You have to give them permission to do what they must to steer you where you need to go.

What Are Angels?

Angels are the highest divine energy beings on Earth. They're so much more than just spirit guides. They're light beings that work within the very core of our souls, guiding and assisting those experiencing spiritual growth. Their purpose is to serve the highest good and justice of all living things, and they do this by teaching people all that they need to know about love and consciousness. They're much more powerful and important than our materialist concept of an angel suggests.

You see, these spiritual allies are guardians we need in our lives to keep us on the right path by standing up for those who can't do it themselves. They're the ones who actually help you make the transition to your next life, so it's in your best interest to work with them regularly. Angels are all thought to be good, loving beings that work for the greater good of the whole human race. There's an endless list of angels out there that is impossible to mention here in one chapter, but the important thing is to do some research and see which one resonates with you the most, checking in with your intuition.

Where Do Angels Come From?

Everyone who knows anything about angels and archangels will tell you they come from the highest point of pure Divine Love. They're the ones closest to the Source Energy of the Universe because they work with this energy daily. When we allow angels to work with us, we become more focused on love and light and start letting go of our fears and troubles because we know it doesn't matter in the grand scheme of things. Our angels always guide us, ensuring we're doing what needs to be done. Because they're so advanced compared to us, they know what's best for us, even if we aren't aware of it.

Do Angels Have a Gender?

When you take a look at the many religious texts that talk about angels, you'll notice that, for the most part, they are described as men. However, this isn't always the case as some of them are women, too. Those of us who have encountered angels in our daily lives know that they come in both genders and in whatever form you find easiest to relate to them in. For instance, Gabriel is a special kind of angel known as an archangel, and he can appear to us as a man or a woman, depending on the situation. The thing about angels, though, is that there are times when they'll show up in a way that makes it difficult and even unnecessary to figure out their gender.

The thing to realize about gender is that it is mostly an earthly concept. In other words, angels do not operate based on the earthly rules and customs we have in place for ourselves, which means they can show up however they want to when they decide to make an appearance on our plane. One might then want to ask, do the angels pick specific genders based on the goals they want to accomplish here? Or is the perception of their gender down to the beliefs and convictions of the people they appear to?

When you check out the Quran, Bible, and Torah, you'll notice that these beings are mostly referred to as predominantly male. However, an interesting bit of scripture in both the Bible and the Torah indicates these religions recognize female angels. Check out the book of Zechariah, chapter five, verses nine to eleven, and you'll note that these scriptures talk about a couple of female angels who raised a basket and a male angel from whom Zechariah received an answer to his question in that passage.

You should also note that angels have energy specific to each gender for specific functions on Earth. Doreen Virtue wrote the Angel Therapy Handbook, and she talks about the fact that while they don't have set genders as their spiritual beings, they do have certain traits and strengths that give them energies you can deduce as very masculine or feminine. For instance, Michael is an archangel known for offering protection, a role primarily thought of as masculine. Then you have Jophiel, who is about beauty, a concept traditionally considered feminine. Despite this, it is important to note that gender-wise, the spirit realm has far more variety than we've already discovered here on Earth.

How Many Angels Are There?

There are as many angels as humans, if not more. It's pretty hard to tell how many exist, and considering that more and more humans are being born every second, it's a fool's errand to figure out how many angels are assigned to each one of us. It's even more pointless when you consider that we could have multiple angels performing different functions on our behalf.

Angelic Hierarchy

There are nine known classes of angels in existence. Note that when it comes to spiritual entities, they go through various cycles of existence, advancing from one level to another, which is why there's a hierarchy to begin with. The higher the rank, the older and wiser the angels, and the closer they are to the energy that creates and sustains worlds. Let's take a look at the rankings.

The seraphim are the highest-ranking angels, and they're known as spirits of love. Everything they do is rooted in the will of the Divine and nothing else. They are also known as the burning ones.

The cherubim are next in line. They're in charge of ensuring a sense of balance and harmony regarding all spiritual consciousness. This is why they're called spirits of harmony. These beings have learned what it means to have Divinely inspired wisdom and knowledge and to recognize the will of Source Energy in one and all.

The thrones are angels who are very aware of Divine Will, in all people and situations, even in what seems less than ideal. They understand that all boundaries and responsibilities have been set in place by the wisdom of the Divine and should not be questioned. They show the Source's brilliance by upholding its will.

The kyriotetes are known as spirits of wisdom. They are all about the expression of Divine Grace and will inspire you to be aware of the infinite possibility that's around you. They're also known as "dominions," in charge of the lower-ranking angels. It's rare to find them mingling with humans. Instead, they'll do their work for you by using a lower-ranked angel as a proxy.

The dynamis are called spirits of motion, and they're well aware of that which needs action that creates change and sustains life. They're all about miracles, and they're known as "Virtues" since they know the connection between having the will to act and the courage to follow through on what needs to be done.

The Elohim are known as spirits of form because they are in charge of all matters involving the incarnation of life on this planet. They have access to the grand blueprint of the Master Architects for every soul, and they're well aware of the precise points in time and space for you to achieve certain milestones meant for the evolution of your soul.

The archaea are spirits of time, and they are the ones who handle the seasons and cycles of the universe and each being.

Sometimes you might hear them as "Principalities" or spirits of personality. It is their task to make sure humanity evolves spiritually on schedule.

The archangels, who we shall soon discuss in detail, are known as spirits of fire. They're in charge of whole nations or collectives of human souls, and they're to space what the archaea is to time. They work as go-betweens for the people and Consciousness or the Divine.

The angels are the final ranking here, and they're the ones we're closest to as humans. Their job is to help us become more aware of our lives and to figure out what it is we came here for, what we must fix by way of karma, and how to attain knowledge of the true nature of reality through dharma. We can work directly with them; we all have at least one angel looking out for our well-being, helping us figure out our consciousness and find the divinity within.

More on Archangels

What is the difference between Angels and Archangels? People tend to use the terms angel and archangel interchangeably, but there's one important difference you should know about. Archangels are much more powerful than the average angel because they're in command of the angels surrounding you daily. For example, Archangel Michael is an archangel who serves as a guardian for the whole human race. He works with his army of angels to deter all evil from entering our world, and he's one of the top angels that people have been able to connect with.

In the Judeo-Christian angelic framework, you have the following archangels as the most important ones:

- Archangel Michael, the warrior
- Archangel Raphael, the healer
- Archangel Gabriel, the messenger
- Archangel Jophiel, in charge of beauty
- Archangel Ariel is in charge of animals and nature
- Archangel Azrael, overseer of death

- Archangel Chamuel is in charge of peace in relationships

In Islam, you have the following major archangels:
- Mikal, the provider
- Jibril, the revealer
- Izra'il, in charge of death.
- Israful, in charge of the final judgment of man

In Occultism, you can call on any of the traditional Judeo-Christian archangels. The idea is that archangels don't have free will, so you can invoke them simply by calling their name and asking them to do whatever you need to be done.

How Angels and Archangels Act as Your Spirit Guides

1. **They keep us safe and protected.** We only have to go back to the Bible in the story of Jacob to know that angels are there for protection and guidance. The most notable instance of angelic protection is when God sent his angel Raphael, a healer, to save a young Tobias and his father from death.

2. **They guide us.** Another important thing we should know is that angels are there with us at all times. They're the ones who give us love and inspiration, and they guide us through the dark days of our lives. They'll always let you know when you need to know if someone is a good person.

3. **They inspire us.** Another thing that angels do is inspire us. When we're down in our emotions or in a bad mood, we can turn to our angels for assistance to get out of that mood. They're the ones who can help us turn things around because they know everything that's happening in our lives. They're the ones who tell us to move forward no matter what. They can also provide insight and advice, so you know that everything you do is the right decision.

4. **They provide spiritual support.** Another thing that angels can do is get spiritual support for you, keep you on track in your life and encourage you when needed. They're the ones who tell you to do everything in your power to make an impact on this world.

How to Connect with Angels and Archangels

1. **Work with your spirit guides daily.** Even if it's only for a few minutes, you can. Your angels and archangels are there to help guide you in the right direction. They can show you what to do and where to go at certain points in your life. They're ripe with wisdom and knowledge, but you must be open enough to hear their guidance. Many people get frustrated when they don't get the desired results, but they need to learn how to be more patient. Our angels are great teachers, so we shouldn't give up on them so easily when they teach us difficult lessons.

2. **Let your angels guide you.** It may be hard at first, but you must learn to trust your guides. They're there for a reason. Follow their lead, even when it doesn't appear to make sense to you. They will take you to a place that could be even better than wherever you wanted to go originally.

3. **Say prayers to them about whatever you need.** Don't just have these beings come into your life and expect them to fix everything on their own. You still have to work with them every day, so you can learn how to get the guidance you need from them. They're always looking out for you, but you have to give yourself to them for them to show you the way, and the best way to achieve this is through conscious prayer to them.

4. **Feel gratitude for your angels.** One of the most important things is to feel a deep sense of appreciation for your guides. When you do this, you're sending out a clear message to the Universe that you want more of the same. The better way to do this is through prayer, just like when you pray to God.

5. **Get rid of all your limits.** Many things will hold you back from connecting with your angels and archangels, but the best way to do this is by having an open mind and being receptive to their guidance.

Chapter Eight: Contact Your Guardian Angel

It is said that everyone has a guardian angel assigned to them at birth. Whether it be a specific person or a more abstract entity, this being will serve as the individual's greatest ally. Angels are said to be able to appear in many forms and to have different duties depending on the person that they are assigned.

But what exactly does an angel represent? The word "angel" means messenger. This may seem like a simple definition, but there is much more here than meets the eye. When Westerners think of angels, they often imagine a being with wings and halos. But this does not accurately reflect the range of beliefs about angels in other cultures.

In Eastern thought, for example, an angel is usually considered to be body-less or even to have several bodies at once. Rather than wings, angels may have long hair or many hands. They also vary in terms of their assigned duties. Some may be messengers while others are warriors, and yet others are servants.

Westerners may also avoid having angels assigned to them before birth and simply believe that angels exist independently, perhaps on some higher plane. But most cultures do not separate their guardian spirits from the world in this way. Unlike Westerners, many Eastern thinkers believe that angels have always been a part of the human world, present on Earth from the beginning of time.

What Is a Guardian Angel?

Angels are considered powerful beings that often inhabit a higher realm and can affect the world below. The ancients believed that they brought them gifts after death. They also sometimes protected humans from dangers, including illnesses and natural disasters. In this sense, they were considered somewhat like guardians or protectors.

They are thought to be able to affect the world in general. Most cultures believe that angels can relax their presence if they like or take on human forms if they want to. But in some cases, they also act as soldiers and messengers. Their duties and purpose vary from culture to culture. But whatever they do and however they appear, they are almost always depicted as benevolent beings who protect the deserving. Even in the case of cultures that don't believe in guardian angels, angels are still assigned to people in the afterlife. These are known as guardian angels.

This is because all humans have souls. A soul is an invisible entity that is unique to each person and carries with it all the individual's knowledge and identity. Souls are also thought to be powerful spirits that can move freely through time and space when released from the physical bondage of the flesh. It used to be thought that the soul was formed at conception. Then, in the 12th century, a monk named Thomas Aquinas argued that it was created at birth. In the 19th and 20th centuries, doctors discovered that around the time of conception comes a special moment when the sperm and egg are most closely joined and can start to carry out their mission. For this reason, some people believe that angels do indeed intervene directly with their help at this stage in their lives.

The medieval theologian, St. Thomas Aquinas, argued that each of us has a guardian angel to watch over us from birth. Some people believe that this angelic being stays with us throughout our whole lives, protecting and guiding us from afar, while others believe that we are assigned new angels at various points in life.

Angels can appear in many forms to help protect the vulnerable and set them onto a path toward the good. They may appear to us as angels, but they may also appear in any number of different forms. For example, many believe that guardian angels can appear as animals. In some cases, these animals are those that are most sacred to the guardian angel's target. So, a cat may be the form chosen by an angel whose charge is a person who loves cats. At other times, the animal form selected by the angel may have no special significance to its charge at all.

Teaching about guardian angels seems superfluous to some people since so much of this information is readily available on the web, in books, or through other media sources. But the tradition of teaching children about their guardian angels dates back to the end of the 19th century. A cardinal in Turin, Italy, is said to have assigned children a specific angel to whom they could write letters with their questions and fears.

Though stories of guardian angels are more widely known today in connection with Christianity, this tradition has its roots in Judaism, which was known as Mal'akh Degadol or "The Great Angel." In fact, most ancient religions believed wholeheartedly in the existence of guardian angels. For example, Arabs believed that an angel named Azrael watched over newborns from birth until death or entrance into heaven. Zoroastrians believed that a spirit known as a Fravashi was assigned to each individual at birth and stayed with them, watching for their well-being as they grew up and helping guide them to heaven. Muslims also believe that everyone has an angel assigned to them at birth. No matter what your religious disposition, the fact is that angels represent a connection to the divine.

Assigning people guardian angels continues to be common among more modern religions, including Islam, Judaism, and Catholicism. However, this practice is not exclusive to any one religion. A guardian angel may be assigned to an individual at almost any stage in their life, even as they grow up and go through different development stages.

Can You Have More Than One Guardian Angel?

There's no denying that many people believe they can connect with their guardian angels and have done so throughout history. In fact, ancient texts contain numerous references to people who claimed they encountered supernatural beings and were guided by them through difficult times in their lives. But the question is, how many of these angels can one have?

There seems to be no limit to the number of guardian angels we can have. Some people say they've had several guardians at once. One person claimed that her guardian angels simultaneously appeared as three real-life beings. Some people have said that every aspect of their lives, from the time of their birth to the things they do in life, is monitored by several guardian angels.

There's no limit to how many guardian angels you may have. Some believe that you can have multiple guardian angels and that each one has an assigned task to protect you in a specific area of your life. Others say several entities work as one, looking after your daily needs and then switching off on different days. You might also have several guardian angels, but they all work with the same purpose to look out for you fairly throughout your life.

Stories about Guardian Angels

Ali's story: *"Here's how my guardian angel helped me to pay my rent. I had been working a stressful job, and on top of that, my landlord decided to increase the rent after I had been there for over a year. I did not have enough money to pay the increase, so I risked losing my apartment. The only way for me to avoid this was for me to find another job. So, as I meditated for two nights about when I would be evicted, I asked my guardian angel for help with the rent. What happened next was astonishing. I started to have feelings that I was going to get a job, a better-paying one. My phone rang, and my friend mentioned that a place was looking for someone with my particular set of skills and that it was urgent. They were going to hire me because my friend had shown them some of my work, and they were impressed. I got a nudge to ask* for advance pay, and they were more than happy to give it, which meant I got to keep my apartment."

Tomiwa's story: "I had been terribly heartbroken from my last relationship, and for about a year or so, I just stayed away from love. Eventually, though, I began to feel a yearning within me to connect with someone romantically, but I didn't want to repeat the same cycle as I did in previous relationships. I sat in meditation night after night for a week, making my intentions to find true love very clear to my guardian angel. One day, a friend invited me out to a party, and I turned them down. However, my guardian angel appeared to me in my dream and said, 'Go to the party and party hard.' I took that as a sign to say yes and have fun. Turns out, I met the love of my life at that party, and we've been together five years. Still going strong. It would never have happened if my guardian angel hadn't been on hand to help me, and I hadn't reached out to them either."

Liza's story: Here's how my guardian angel saved me from being mugged on the street. Last night I was walking on the street, and a man appeared in front of me. He raised his hand as if he was going to hit me, but before he could make contact with my head, a bright white light emerged from behind him.

He was shocked by it, and his hand went down immediately to his side. The light then moved toward me and encircled my body. I could feel something warm moving around my body and then down into the earth below me. I felt myself being lifted off the ground and carried upwards to who knows where.

The whole time, I could hear the man who had tried to accost me calling out to anyone who could hear him, asking what that light was doing there and where it had come from. I stood rooted to the spot, confused and a bit shaken but otherwise unharmed. I heard a soft voice say to me, "You're safe now." If you'd asked me where the owner of that voice was, I really wouldn't have been able to tell you because it was only the man and me on that silent, lonely, poorly lit street. That's when I looked down at my feet and saw the man who had tried to mug me lying unconscious where I had once been standing. I knew then and there that I'd been kept safe by my guardian angel. To this day, I do not take the connection I have with my angel for granted. They've done so *many awesome things for me that it's truly hard to keep track of it all."*

Signs Your Guardian Angel Is Near

1. **You hear your name being whispered in your ear in the middle of the night or early in the morning.** If you've ever experienced this before, and it left you frightened, don't be. This is likely your guardian angel trying to let you know that they know who you are. They know your struggles and needs and are more than happy to assist you. They call your name to help you realize the truth that you're never alone, even at your worst.

2. **You see a bright light in your room.** Many people believe that when you see this, it's your guardian angel calling for your attention. They want you to know that they're always watching over you and can be seen by you if you wish.

3. **You hear someone call out to you during the day while doing your thing.** In the past, people have reported hearing angelic choirs singing and whispering in other languages. These signs are indications that your guardian angels are near, trying to get your attention and let you know they're present.

4. **You feel angels around.** Do you ever feel like someone's standing right behind or above your shoulder? This is a common sign of them trying to get your attention.

5. **You have dreams of talking with your guardian angels.** Some people regularly dream of their guardians, insisting they're real. This is a sign that you've successfully connected with your guardian angel, and they're trying to communicate with you on the other side. They may want to tell you something important or warn you of something coming around the corner.

6. **You start to notice more synchronicity in your life.** It's said that when you're connected with your guardian angel, there are more synchronicities than ever before in your life. These experiences can include conversations, seeing signs and messages, hearing voices, or seeing images.

Sometimes they can be coincidences that aren't really significant on their own. Other experiences are very real and significant

Ways to Contact Your Guardian Angel

Today, there are many practices that people go through to establish contact with their guardian angels. Let's look at some of these methods.

Meditation. Meditating on your guardian angel's energy or connecting with them is more than enough to help you establish contact and begin working with them. You could fix an image of them in your mind as you breathe with your eyes shut in meditation. Alternatively, you could chant their name in your head or out loud or keep your eyes open while focusing on a picture of them if you can draw or paint them. To use meditation to contact guardian angels, first, you will need to decide on your work's specific intention and outcome. You may want to ask the angels for protection from harm, healing from a disease or condition, guidance, and direction in life, help with a career choice, etc. You will then want to connect with your own emotions and commit to yourself that you will do what it takes to achieve your chosen outcome. After this, you can then sit in meditation, breathe, and try to open up your heart and mind to feel your angels' presence.

Channeling or mediumship. One of the most popular methods for contacting guardian angels is said to be mediumship or channeling, a practice in which people believe that they can use their mind or body as a channel for communicating directly with spirits from another realm. The medium channeling process usually involves an individual sitting in a darkened room and channeling thoughts and images projected through their spirit guide's hands. These messages may be delivered through movement, sounds, speech, colorful lights, or even bodily tics.

Prayer. Another popular technique for communicating with guardian angels is through prayer, a common practice for many cultures throughout history. The practice of prayer is generally understood as a spiritual concept, as it involves putting one's thoughts into words and physically speaking to the spirits of the heavenly realm. This is done by speaking to the angels in their minds or out loud, reading prayers out loud, or praying silently. Sometimes, people request permission from their guardian angels to pray aloud on behalf of others.

Chapter Nine: Working with Archangels

It is known that archangels have a lot more power and dominion than angels, and they all have their assigned purpose given to them by the Divine. For instance, Michael is charged with protecting one and all, Raphael is the one who heals, and Gabriel is very helpful when dealing with communication matters, passing along clear messages, and so on. So, in this chapter, we'll take a look at the roles played by each archangel and explain how they can help you in your personal life. *Note: Remember that some are gendered as female and some as male, but it's notable that different belief systems use different genders for some angels. We've used the most common gender for each archangel listed below.*

Archangel Michael

This is the one archangel who is recognized in the sacred texts of Christianity, Judaism, and Islam. This angel is a protector and will always go to war against all that is evil. Archangel Michael is a very powerful being. As long as you have a pure heart and good intentions, he will definitely fight for you when you need him to. He is all about preserving truth – and cannot stand it when people get away with wickedness and injustice to the undeserving. When you get in touch with Michael, you will find his energy is bold and unmistakable. When he communicates with you, he does so with clarity, so you can't miss his message.

Signs Archangel Michael Is Present

You get help when you're in trouble. The divine dispatches this archangel to help you whenever you're in a tight or desperate situation that feels like a real crisis. Many people know you can call on this archangel whenever you're in trouble, and you'll get help immediately. It doesn't matter what you need protection from. He never shies away from lovingly coming to your aid.

He also has an energy that seeps into you, infusing your body, mind, and soul with a sense of calm even in the face of danger. He'll fuel you with the strength to handle whatever comes your way and the courage you need to handle things. Some can actually perceive his aura when he comes around. It's a lovely shade of royal purple, reminiscent of cobalt blue. Others report hearing his voice with their actual ears rather than on the inside.

Regardless of how this archangel shows up, it's often unmistakable when he's in the building. You will see actual evidence, as he's big on making it clear that he's around. You'll also find that there are times he will choose to communicate through your intuition.

You feel a sense of reassurance. If you're in a pickle and need to feel encouraged, Michael will turn up if you call on him. You may notice you're getting an image of him in your head or that you feel a warm, comforting sensation when he shows up. All of these serve to reassure you that you're not alone. He also shows up to comfort those who are about to pass on to the afterlife.

You're driven to accomplish your life purpose. You'll find this archangel is invested in helping you organize your life and boost your productivity levels. You'll know he's with you when you notice that you're leveling up your skills, which helps get you where you need to be. He will help you be more consistent in your efforts.

He will guide you in your dreams. He will sometimes appear in your dreams to give you the guidance that you seek on any matter. Often, you'll know he's there by the appearance of flashes of light.

Archangel Raphael

He is one of the most popular and well-known archangels among Jewish people. He hasn't just been mentioned in the Hebrew Bible but also in later writings as well. His role is to heal and protect people, animals, and even plants. When seeking healing, you can call Archangel Raphael for assistance. This archangel will heal you from both physical and emotional pain. He'll even help you get rid of your fear.

Signs Archangel Raphael Is Present

You feel lighter, happier, and calmer. When you're feeling really stressed out, depressed, or afraid to get up in the morning, this archangel will show up to give you the energy boost that you need. He'll clear and energize your body and mind, making you feel brand-new. His light will fill you with positive energy and the hope that things will be okay.

The presence of the Archangel Raphael will allow you to feel happier and calmer. .
https://pixabay.com/images/id-591576/

You notice that something in your life is changing for the better. If it's been a while since something good has happened to you in your personal life, this archangel will make sure he's there to help guide you through this period. He wants to help you reach your full potential, live your best life, and work out any problems you may face. He will come up with a solution that works perfectly for you at the moment that you need it most.

He guides you in your dreams. When he's around, this archangel will appear to you in your dreams to guide you on matters of the heart. He'll tell you how to get back into a better love relationship or patch things up with someone important to you. He knows the right words to say so that everyone can have a perfect outcome.

Archangel Gabriel

This archangel has been mentioned in many popular movies and books. He is represented as being both powerful and beautiful. He is a messenger from God and a healer who will help you recover from hard times.

Signs Archangel Gabriel Is Present

You are inspired to put things into motion. This archangel will help you get started with the action you want to take in your life - whether that means starting a business or making the changes that will turn your dreams into reality. If you're having trouble making decisions, this angel will make sure that you take the first step toward what you've chosen. She knows you can take control of your life and make it amazing, and he wants to coach you in your pursuits.

You get a sense of hope. You feel inspired by this archangel's presence. He loves helping those who are down and out or feel at a dead end in their lives. He knows exactly how you feel when things aren't going your way, so you can tune into his energy and feel good about yourself.

He guides you in your dreams. This angel will guide you in your dreams to help you make the right personal and professional decisions. He'll also tell you how to overcome your fears and get over your obstacles.

Archangel Jophiel

This archangel is in charge of beauty in all its forms, positivity, and creativity. He teaches us how to use our hearts and minds to see the good in others and in ourselves.

Signs Archangel Jophiel Is Present

You feel inspired to follow your passion. You have a burning desire to make your abilities known, whether that means starting a new business, performing on stage, or writing a book. This archangel will show you how you can accomplish all of those things with your natural talents, which are meant for more than just general creativity.

You feel happy. You find yourself doing things that make you smile - even if they're small things, like buying flowers or baking a cake. This angel helps people recognize their worth by helping them find joy in their everyday lives.

You enjoy making others feel good. This archangel will show you how to help others feel better about themselves. He loves taking the time to teach people how to enjoy the simple pleasures of life.

Archangel Ariel

This archangel is in charge of nature and animals. She inspires you to be closer to nature and help animals and the environment. She is there to help you connect with all living things.

Signs Archangel Ariel Is Present

You feel a strong connection to nature. This angel will help you do things that will make you feel closer to the natural world. You may spend more time outside or encourage your family and friends to connect more with the Earth. You don't have to be a vegan or an extreme eco-warrior to tap into her energy; this angel simply wants you to appreciate nature.

You want to be kinder to animals. Whether it's adopting a new pet or working on behalf of animal rights, this archangel will show you how you can make the world a better place for animals. She's there to help you decide to do the right thing for these creatures who don't have a voice of their own.

You want to live more healthily. If you're having trouble sticking with a health plan or eating healthy meals, this angel will inspire you to make it happen through your own willpower. She knows that it takes hard work, determination, and perseverance to be successful in anything you do, but she'll help you through the tough times by reminding you why it's so important for your life.

Archangel Azrael

This angel is in charge of death. He guides people to the afterlife, making sure those who die are ready for their transition.

Signs Archangel Azrael Is Present

You feel at peace with the future. This angel encourages you to rest in your final days and be at peace with what life has had to offer you. You may find yourself reminiscing on your life, which allows you to appreciate the good times and leave them all behind, making your transition easier. You may also cling to the past and have a hard time leaving it behind, but this angel will guide you into thinking about where life might go and help you stay on track.

You are dealing with a death or loss. This angel will give you a sense of peace and closure so that you can move past your grief. He knows it's not easy to deal with loss, but he'll give you the courage and compassion you need to heal.

You feel like life is worth living. This archangel will help you keep pushing forward when life seems hopeless. He knows how hard it can be to keep going when things continue to seem like a struggle, but he'll help guide you toward your goals without giving up hope for better days.

Archangel Chamuel

This archangel is in charge of peaceful relationships between one and all. He brings harmony to people who are struggling with discord.

Signs Archangel Chamuel Is Present

You feel more connected to others. This angel will help you feel less alone and more like you belong in the world. He will help you connect with others and show you that everyone is on your side, even if it doesn't seem that way.

You forgive others. Anyone who someone has ever wronged can tap into this archangel's energy. He encourages us to let go of our anger and resentment to find peace with the ones we love or even forgive those who have hurt us in the past.

You have a new outlook on life. It can be hard to see the good in others when you've been angry or hurt for so long. When this angel is around, you'll feel motivated to start fresh and see the beauty in the world around you. You'll be able to let go of your resentment and see things differently, which will help your relationships grow.

Archangel Jeremiel

This archangel is in charge of wisdom and understanding. He helps us find clarity in our lives by teaching us how to face our fears, overcome our obstacles, and deal with negativity. He's there to help us prepare for life's inevitable challenges and take them head-on.

Signs Archangel Jeremiel Is Present

You feel inspired and motivated to achieve your goals. This angel wants you to be clear on what you want out of life, and he'll help you take a step in the right direction to succeed in the end. He'll give you the courage you need and show you how to face everything head-on, either with a smile or crying because it was so hard.

You recognize your fears. You may find yourself dealing with fears or insecurities, but this angel will show you how to overcome them by facing your fears head-on.

You face your obstacles. This angel is here to help you deal with anything that may be standing in your way of reaching your goals. He'll inspire you to be brave when you're afraid and teach you how to rise above any obstacle that lies in the path of what you want.

Archangel Sandalphon

In charge of music, this angel helps us make music in our lives. He guides us to find the harmony that allows us to make beautiful music.

Signs Archangel Sandalphon Is Present

You learn how to play an instrument. If you haven't learned an instrument yet, this angel will show you how easy it can be to pick up one. He'll also teach you about the different types of music so that deciding on what instrument you want to learn will be easy.

You are inspired to create. This archangel is in charge of making music in your life - whether it's a song, art, or dance - he'll help you bring your creative side out with every project. You may be working on an art project or writing lyrics for a new song. This angel will help you bring it all together and make something beautiful or move out of it.

You feel like you can weather the storm. This archangel is here to guide you through any storm life throws. He'll help you find the positive in life's hardships so that you'll dance with them gracefully.

Archangel Seraphiel

This is the archangel of prayer and purification. He helps us cleanse the body and mind when they are negativity-filled.

Signs Archangel Seraphiel Is Present

You are feeling cleansed and purified. This angel is there to purify your body and mind so that you'll feel renewed and ready to face every day. He'll help you rid your body of impurities and teach you how to keep impurities out through a good diet, positive thinking, and regular prayers.

You are praying more. This angel is there to support your prayers. He wants you to find peace with your dreams and desires so that you can reach out to God and ask for what you need in life. He's there to remind you of the power of prayer and that a higher power is helping you achieve your goals.

You can use your abilities for the greater good. Seraphiel is the angel of prayer, so he's there to help you find a powerful prayer life. He'll teach you how to pray more passionately than ever, leading you to holiness. You may have already had a prayer life before, but things will change dramatically once this angel enters your presence.

You have more energy. This angel will help you feel like you have more energy throughout the day to make the most out of your time. He'll encourage you to get up and keep going, so that life will be more enjoyable for you.

You feel less stressed. When you're feeling overwhelmed or stressed, this archangel will guide you toward a peaceful state of mind where nothing feels overwhelming anymore.

You are more clear-headed. When negativity takes over your mind, it can be hard to focus on anything else.

Archangel Raziel

This is the archangel of secrets, knowledge, and wisdom. He helps us uncover the secrets that are hidden in our lives so that we can uncover our inner wisdom and find true happiness.

Signs Archangel Raziel Is Present

You are drawn to hidden treasures. This angel is in charge of finding the gifts that come from keeping your eyes and ears open. He will help you see things in new ways to look at your life with a different set of eyes. He will teach you how to uncover treasures and valuable knowledge that you wouldn't see otherwise, which can lead to personal growth and change for the better.

You gain inner strength. You may have moments when it feels like the walls are closing in on you, but this archangel will help pull back those walls and give you the strength to move forward, even through the hardest times.

You awaken your inner wisdom. This angel will inspire you to look deeper into yourself and find your inner truth. Your knowledge might be greater than you realize, but this angel will help you recognize what's within your own mind.

You feel more fulfilled. It can be hard to get back on track whenever we're not happy with ourselves or feel a lack of fulfillment in our lives. This angel will help you get out of whatever rut you've fallen into and inspire you to find more fulfillment in your life.

How to Call on Archangels to Help You

1. **Say a prayer to them.** If you've never called on an archangel before, say a short prayer to them and ask them to fill your life with their presence.
2. **Ask for help.** Tell them what you need, and ask them to guide you toward it.
3. **Visualize.** While you are praying or asking for help, visualize yourself in a peaceful place and see them coming to visit you there. Tell them all you want to, trust that they've heard you, and you will receive an answer soon.
4. **Feel their love.** While calling upon your angels, allow yourself to feel the wave of love they give into the world. It will lift your spirits as they enter your heart and soul.
5. **Be grateful.** Say a thank-you prayer, and be grateful for everything that is going on in your life.
6. **Believe.** Trust that they will help you and remind you of their power to guide you toward a better life because they do.

How to Show Archangels You Honor Them

1. **Thank them.** Thank them for the gifts that they've given you and the blessings bestowed upon your life.
2. **Ask to serve.** Ask these angels to guide you toward serving others and bringing joy into people's lives. They will help you every step, bringing more joy into your life.
3. **Give thanks.** Give thanks for all of their help because it is their gift to you.
4. **Respect their presence within your life.** Take a moment each day to contemplate the archangels' presence, all they've done for you, and the fact that they have never let you down.

Doing these things will not only show them you value them but will guarantee that it's easier for you to connect with them each time you need them and get even faster and more dramatic results from drawing on their energy in your life.

Chapter Ten: Other Guides and How to Find Them

There are other beings that you can communicate and work with besides the ones we've mentioned in this book so far. Among them are plants, mythical creatures, star beings, and so on. So, without further ado, let's discuss all the other kinds of spirit guides and explain how you can work with them.

Plants as Spirit Guides

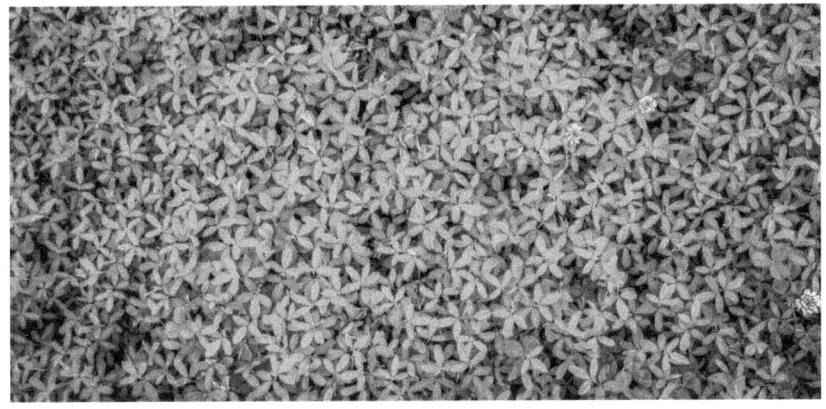

Plants can also be spirit guides.
https://pixabay.com/images/id-1498985

Can a plant be your spirit guide? Many believe that plants are your first spirit guides. After all, it was in nature that humans grew and developed a connection with the world around them. The plants within nature can be seen as a form of spirit guide for everyone because they have a sense of awareness and can communicate with you.

Some plants can also be used in nature magic spells, and that's because they have their own spirit with their own deep knowledge and wisdom, which could benefit you immensely, both physically and spiritually. If you are looking for a plant spirit guide to communicate with, you can use any plant that you like or work with the ones that call to you specifically.

There's nothing weird about being spiritually guided by a plant. Just because it remains rooted to a spot doesn't mean it's not very alive and sentient. This is an ideology rooted in plant spirit shamanism. Shamans know that plants have power and can act as a connection between the physical and spiritual worlds.

Plant spirit shamanism was practiced by the ancients and continues to be practiced today. Often, you can work with plants to help you heal your mind and body. To connect with the plants as spirit guides, you must learn to listen to their call. That's right. Plants actually speak to us. You'll realize this if you learn to pay attention.

Zion's story: *"Here's how a plant spirit guide helped me reconcile with my family once more. I had spent most of my life as a loner because of a terrible incident in my family where I was falsely accused of something I didn't do and therefore ostracized. I couldn't look at them in the same way ever again, especially since I saw them as evil. I soon cut myself off from the family because there was no other way for me to deal with them.*

After years of being totally estranged from some members of my family, I thought they were still stuck in the same cycle of dysfunction, and it didn't matter what either of us did or said to change that. Sadly, some family members continued to do the same thing, and I hated them even more.

This is how I spent my life. Every day was filled with memories of pain. I couldn't get away from the pain of my past, but that changed when I chose to connect with a plant spirit guide, and I met her in my dream. Her name was Elsie. She showed me how to connect with the world around me in a way that no other person had ever done before.

Elsie was my first plant spirit guide because she brought me into a whole new arena of consciousness and spirituality that opened up a new way for me to see life itself. I discovered that I could see the world as a spiritual phenomenon and that I wasn't stuck in a cycle of pain. As I learned more about myself and began using different plants as spirit guides to heal my mind and body, my life began to change for the better.

It was at this time when I met Elsie, and things started to get better for me. She helped me realize that not all people on this planet are bad and that many of them came here with good intentions. In fact, they came here seeking opportunities because they believed they could improve their lives through knowledge. With time, she began to share insight about my family, and she showed me who the culprit was that had sown discord between them and me. She even showed me where to look for proof I could use to exonerate myself. After years of being cut off, I reached out with this proof, and everyone realized their mistake. We came together, reconciled our differences, and now I have a love for my family once more."

Working with Plant Spirit Guides

1. **Spend more time in nature:** Doing this will make it possible for you to hear the trees and other plants around you. Walk around nature to hear the plants calling to you, and they will. Be very clear about your intention, and you should find yourself a plant spirit friend in no time.

2. **Connect your consciousness with that of the plant.** You can do this by tuning your senses to pay attention to the various qualities contained within the plant, as well as the healing power it has. You can do this by mindfully observing the plant by gazing at it. As you look, allow your heart to fully open up to the plant. Feel nothing but love, and wait expectantly.

3. **Treat the plants lovingly.** You should have respect for the plants. When you do, they're more willing to work with you. So, ensure you revere them by leaving them undisturbed rather than picking at them unnecessarily. You can even say some loving, kind words to the plant to develop a relationship with its spirit. When that relationship is thriving, you can ask it what you will, and it will gladly show up for you in the best way it can.

Mythological Creatures as Spirit Guides

Don't let the fact that these creatures come from "myths" and myths are supposedly not true stop you from seeking a connection to them. The fact that we have these stories means that the consciousnesses of these creatures are very real indeed. The mythologies surrounding creatures like the mermaid, centaur, gorgon, and others will reveal much about their characters, letting you know who would be the best creature to work with to get results.

Now let's talk about these trans-species, which are part human, part beast. Whether it's a sphinx, harpy, faun, Minotaur, or fairy, it doesn't matter who you choose to work with as long as their energy matches yours. How will you know? It will feel right, and your intuition will confirm that you should be working with the being. Let's take a look at some of these creatures.

The centaur is famous, with a man's head and torso and a horse's legs and flank. Centaurs are powerful. They are fierce guardians of the wild spirit and the land and provide stability wherever they go. Centaurs can be fierce if you provoke them, but they are also very compassionate. The centaur has the strength of a man with the wisdom of a horse.

The fairy is another famous creature that commonly appears in folklore. Fairies are incredibly playful beings that love being in nature, roaming the earth, and playing tricks on humans to make them happy. Fairies also have a natural connection with healing because their energies align well with nature and herbs, trees, flowers, and water. All fairies love music, for it brings out their natural creative energy.

The gorgons happen to be sisters from Greek mythology. Their names are Stheno, Euryale, and Medusa, the latter being the most popular of the bunch. The thing about them is that they were totally human – except for the fact that instead of hair, they had a mass of hissing snakes that writhed about on their heads. They were scary because to look upon them directly meant you'd be turned into stone in a heartbeat. Their energy can be very useful when you want to freeze an enemy who has been bugging you unnecessarily in their tracks.

The mandrake is a combination of humans and plants. It's also a set of plants you can find in the Mediterranean, and the interesting thing about them is that their roots resemble an actual face. Also, this plant is a known hallucinogen, which just adds to its lore. It's said that the plant has a scream so loud when it's dug up from the earth that anyone within earshot will die instantly. You may remember this from a certain popular movie franchise based on a series of magical books.

The mermaid is popular, with a woman's torso and head and a fish's lower body. This mythological creature has its roots in Assyria, from ancient times. It is said that Atargatis, the goddess, had been terribly ashamed because she was responsible for the death of her lover, who was human. To punish herself, she chose to turn herself into a mermaid. Since this time, many tales have been told about this creature, and some swear they have met them.

The selkie has Scottish and Irish roots, being half woman and half seal.

The Minotaur is half man, half bull, and etymologically, its name is based on Minos, a bull god of Crete, specifically the Minoans. Minos was also a king who demanded to be fed meals made by the youth of Athens.

The satyr is of Greek origin, and this creature is half man, half goat. The Roman version is known as the faun. It's relatively safe, except around women. This being is devoted to hedonism and wants nothing more than sheer pleasure, no matter how it gets it.

The siren is also from Greece mythology. Its torso and head are human, and it has a bird's tail and legs. This was not a creature sailors ever wanted to meet on their voyages because it most certainly meant doom, a gloomy, watery death for all who would hear her seductive tune lulling them onto dangerous reefs. Homer wrote an epic known as "The Odyssey," and here, when Odysseus was making his way back from Troy, he had to have himself tied securely to the ship's mast so that he wouldn't give in to the siren's melodies.

The sphinx has a human head and a lion's body. Sometimes, you'll see it depicted with an eagle's wings and a snake's tail. This is rooted in ancient Egyptian mythology on account of the Giza sphinx. It was also in Greek mythology. Each time it shows up in a story, danger comes. It will ask humans to answer tough questions, which, when not answered correctly, would cause it to devour them angrily. This was also a creature that played a role in Oedipus's story. Oedipus gave the Sphinx a correct answer, but he had to pay the price. The Greek myths hold that the head of a sphinx is a woman's, while the Egyptian ones insist it's a man.

Which Creature Should You Work With?

One thing you can do to figure things out is to think about the attributes of the animals that these creatures have as part of who they are. Would you like to channel the bravery and ruthlessness of a lion? Perhaps you should work with the sphinx. You should also consider what each creature is known for. Would you like to work some sweet magic where you're sweet in your methods but get deadly, effective results? The siren is a good pick. Want to find a way to forgive yourself for some wrong you did in the past? Then how about working with the mermaid? It's all down to you.

On the other hand, don't assume your choice has to make sense. You can pick one, work with it, and see the results you get. If you're not getting anything useful, try another. Eventually, you'll land upon what you should work with.

Another way to pick would be to choose the ones that resonate with your preferred gender or the ones that your ancestors thought were worth their time and effort. You could check in with your other guides to see what's right for you, use a pendulum as we've talked about in an earlier chapter, or ask that they reveal themselves to you as you go to bed at night.

Star Beings

These are other civilizations in the stars and not part of the human race. It is believed that among regular humans, some of us are star seeds, which means we incarnated here from one of the star systems to fulfill some mission on this Earth. Let's take a look at some of these beings in detail.

Pleiadians. Pleiadians are a group of collective consciousness extraterrestrial beings who have intervened in human events for the last twenty-five thousand years. They hail from the Pleiadian star system called Pleiades, one of the oldest in our galaxy, bearing seven planets called the Seven Sisters inhabited by their own kind and other life forms. They are here to assist humanity, who is living through a great transformation at this time.

We have had many experiences in which Pleiadians helped us and communicated with us, sometimes while we were awake and aware that they were present, while at other times while we were asleep, dreaming what seemed to be normal human dreams. Their civilizations have thrived for hundreds of thousands, if not millions, of years. They were likely the first to contact Earth at some point in antiquity, often humanoid in appearance and communicating by telepathy. They keep records on behalf of the earth, have advanced and rapid healing abilities, and are interested in all those who want to grow in consciousness.

Sirians: The Sirians are a collective of beings from the Sirius star system. The Sirians have coexisted with Earth and our Solar System for eons. There is evidence that the Sirian systems have been manipulated and seeded by a larger collective of beings who use the Draco and Orion star systems as their "farmland," so to speak. The entities who manage the Draco and Orion systems are typically (but not necessarily) reptilian in nature, while those in Sirius are humanoid.

Sirius is a star that is less than nine light-years from Earth, making it the second-closest star to us. It's the brightest star in the sky and the only one named after a living being, the Dog Star. Sirius has at least two giant planets believed to be about the size of Jupiter and possibly other planets. Like our Sun, Sirius has a companion star — a white dwarf called Sirius B (the "Pup"). This partner star revolves around Sirius relatively rapidly, completing an orbit in just 50 years. Sirians are the ones who keep the peace and guard the world, so it's safe for us all.

Arcturians: Arcturian aliens are a collective of beings from the Arcturus star system. They are sometimes collectively referred to as the Tall Whites by some. Arcturians have visited Earth occasionally but prefer to remain in the background where they can observe without interference.

The name "Arcturians" is also used to describe an intelligent species native to Arcturus's four gas giant planets. These planets were seeded with life by a race of Zeta Reticuli-type beings who arrived there from Sirius C in our solar system thousands of years ago. The Arcturian system is about 36.7 light-years from Earth and has a planet very similar to Earth. At this time, approximately 150 million beings are living in the Arcturian realm at any one time. They were among the very first races in our galaxy to achieve galactic travel, and they originated in a star system called Alpha Centauri, four light-years away from ours. These beings have a strong will, are natural leaders, and are the ones we can credit for building the world.

Andromedans: Andromedans are a collective consciousness extraterrestrial race living on and visiting Earth for at least thousands of years. They are one of the most advanced races in our galaxy and have been here to assist humanity, who is living through a great transformation at this time. They require highly evolved spiritually as well as technologically.

The Andromedan race originated in our own galaxy, where they advanced spiritually and technologically far beyond their ancestors. As revealed in some unidentified ancient texts, they arrived here at the same time that Earth's dinosaurs became extinct, roughly 65 million years ago, which alters the conventional explanation for the demise of those creatures (which is usually attributed to a meteor strike). They alone know what their purpose is, but they're great at accessing the akashic records, where everything that has ever happened or will ever happen is stored.

Orions: The Orion Alliance is a collective of beings from the Orion star system. They are sometimes collectively referred to as the Tall Whites by some. A maverick group of ancient civilizations, they think and act very differently from us. They often don't communicate to us in our own language but through symbols that we recognize but don't consciously think about. They do their best to protect Earth and humanity. Still, they can be a little too controlling at times, which is why they use negative manipulation on certain individuals or groups on Earth who have not yet learned how to free themselves from these influences. They want to improve our science and technology, and they want to help us see the potential we have.

Lemurians and Atlanteans: Lemuria and Atlantis were one and the same. Eventually, both cultures split into two groups: those who wanted to return to the past and those who wanted to bring in the new age. Those who wished to return to Lemuria created the Bermuda Triangle, a place to escape or draw energy. Atlanteans had better technology than our own, and they could bring a lot of energy to the planet. Atlantis was indeed an advanced society that thrived for thousands of years.

Lyrans: Lyrans are a collective of beings from the Lyran star system. They have coexisted with Earth and our Solar System for eons. The Lyran system has a planet very similar to Earth. At this time, several hundred thousand beings are living in the Lyran realm at any one time. They were among the very first races in our galaxy to achieve galactic travel, and they originated in a star system called Vega. We have to thank these beings for creating fire and humanity itself.

How to Contact These Spirit Guides

1. **Reach out to your guides by scrying.** Scrying involves gazing into a crystal or other reflective object and seeing images that can help you communicate with them. You can create a quick reflective surface by filling a dark bowl with water in a dark room, lighting a candle, and then staring into the water until things begin to reveal themselves. Don't force yourself to see what isn't there. Spend 15 minutes per session, and don't be upset if you see nothing the first few times. Something will come to you eventually.

2. **Make an altar.** If you want to contact your guides, make an altar where they can sit and reveal themselves to you. An easy way to do this is to create a small table with images of the beings you want to contact and a candle.
3. **Meditate.** Keep the essence of the being on your mind as you do so.
4. **Visualize.** See these beings in your mind's eye during your meditation.
5. **Try Bibliomancy.** This means using random passages from the Bible to glean information from these beings. You can simply open your Bible or any other book to a random page and read the first thing your eyes fall on. Note what that is because if the meaning isn't clear to you at first, it will be much later.

Conclusion

You've finally come to the end of this book, and it's been quite a trip. You now have all the information you need to begin communicating with your guides. Before wrapping this up, it's worth making it very clear that it's one thing to read about your guides and another thing entirely to develop a relationship with them. Just because you know it doesn't mean they'll show up automatically. You have to be the one to reach out and make it clear to them that you're ready and can develop something serious with them.

It should also be stated for the record that this is a matter of constant practice. In other words, just because something phenomenal hasn't happened since you began meditating or visualizing for a week or two doesn't mean you should quit. Think of this less as some quick fix to handle your life problems and more as a lifestyle. It's a great idea to pick a specific time of day or night to practice what you must connect with your guides. When you make a habit of it, it becomes a ritual, priming the pump so that you and your spirit guides can bridge the divide between you and begin to work together meaningfully.

Please be very wary about preparing and staying safe before performing any spiritual exercises. The last thing you want is to attract a mischievous spirit masquerading as the deity or being you want to connect with. So, take your time cleansing yourself. Clear the clutter in your mind and in your meditation space, too. Make sure your intention is very strong about who it is you want to reach out to, and you should be just fine.

While it's okay to ask your guides for things, please don't just reach out only when you need help. You should commune with them, honor them, and say hello, just because. Think about it. You don't like it when people only reach out when they need things, do you? Well, your guides aren't any different. You want to have a relationship with them, not just transactions. They began to bless me beyond my wildest dreams when I became intentional about connecting with them and honoring them without expecting anything in return. Sometimes they're the ones reaching out to me. Now that's the sort of relationship worth having with beings that know more than you and love you more than anyone else could. I wish you good luck on your spiritual journey. Have fun getting to know your guides.

Here's another book by Silvia Hill that you might like

Free Bonus from Silvia Hill available for limited time

Hi Spirituality Lovers!

My name is Silvia Hill, and first off, I want to THANK YOU for reading my book.

Now you have a chance to join my exclusive spirituality email list so you can get the ebooks below for free as well as the potential to get more spirituality ebooks for free! Simply click the link below to join.

P.S. Remember that it's 100% free to join the list.

~~$27~~ FREE BONUSES

- 9 Types of Spirit Guides and How to Connect to Them
- How to Develop Your Intuition: 7 Secrets for Psychic Development and Tarot Reading
- Tarot Reading Secrets for Love, Career, and General Messages

Access your free bonuses here
https://livetolearn.lpages.co/spirit-guides-paperback/

References

Andrews, T. (1992). How to meet & work with spirit guides. Llewellyn Worldwide.

Blumenthal, S. (1990). Spotted Cattle and Deer: Spirit Guides and Symbols of Endurance and Healing in" Ceremony. "American Indian Quarterly.

Ching, E. D., & Ching, K. (2006). Faces of your soul: Rituals in art, mask making, and guided imagery with ancestors, spirit guides, and totem animals. North Atlantic Books.

Farmer, S. D. (2012). Pocket Guide to Spirit Animals: Understanding Messages from Your Animal Spirit Guides. Hay House, Inc.

Dominguez, I. (2008). Spirit Speak: Knowing and Understanding Spirit Guides, Ancestors, Ghosts, Angels, and the Divine. Red Wheel/Weiser.

Elder, P. (2005). Eyes of an Angel: Soul Travel, Spirit Guides, Soul Mates, and the Reality of Love. Hampton Roads Publishing.

Farmer, S. D. (2006). Animal Spirit Guides: An easy-to-use handbook for identifying and understanding your power animals and animal spirit helpers. Hay House, Inc.

Farmer, S. D. (2012). Pocket Guide to Spirit Animals: Understanding Messages from Your Animal Spirit Guides. Hay House, Inc.

Fisher, J. (2001). The Siren Call of Hungry Ghosts: A Riveting Investigation into Channeling and Spirit Guides. Cosimo, Inc.

Goodare, J. (2020). Emotional relationships with spirit guides in early modern Scotland. In The supernatural in early modern Scotland (pp. 39-54). Manchester University Press.

Jacobs, C. F. (1989). Spirit guides and possession in the New Orleans black spiritual churches. Journal of American folklore.

Marciniak, B. (1992). Bringers of the Dawn: Teachings from the Pleiadians. Simon and Schuster.

Porter, J. E. (1996). Spiritualists, Aliens, and UFOs: Extraterrestrials as spirit guides. Journal of Contemporary Religion.

Webster, R. (1998). Spirit Guides & Angel Guardians: Contact Your Invisible Helpers. Llewellyn Worldwide.

www.ingramcontent.com/pod-product-compliance
Lightning Source LLC
Chambersburg PA
CBHW070340010526
44107CB00004B/572